BEST OF

Valencia

Miles Roddis

How to use this book

Colour-Coding & Maps

Each chapter has a colour code along the banner at the top of the page which is also used for text and symbols on maps (eg all venues reviewed in the Highlights chapter are orange on the maps). The fold-out maps inside the front and back covers are numbered from 1 to 4. All sights and venues in the text have map references; eg (1, A3) means Map 1, grid reference A3. See p96 for map symbols.

Prices

Multiple prices listed with reviews (eg €10/5) usually indicate adult/concession admission to a venue. Concession prices can include senior, student, member or coupon discounts. Meal cost and room rate categories are listed at the start of the Eating and Sleeping chapters, respectively.

Text Symbols

- ☎ telephone
- ✉ address
- 🖳 email/website address
- € admission
- 🕒 opening hours
- ⓘ information
- 🚌 bus
- Ⓜ metro
- 🚆 train
- 🚋 tram
- Ⓟ parking available
- ♿ wheelchair access
- 🍽 on-site/nearby eatery
- 👶 child-friendly venue
- Ⓥ good vegetarian selection

Best of Valencia
1st edition – May 2006

Published by Lonely Planet Publications Pty Ltd
ABN 36 005 607 983

Australia	Head Office, Locked Bag 1, Footscray, Vic 3011 ☎ 03 8379 8000, fax 03 8379 8111 🖳 talk2us@lonelyplanet.com.au
USA	150 Linden St, Oakland, CA 94607 ☎ 510 893 8555, toll free 800 275 8555 fax 510 893 8572 🖳 info@lonelyplanet.com
UK	72–82 Rosebery Ave, Clerkenwell, London EC1R 4RW ☎ 020 7841 9000, fax 020 7841 9001 🖳 go@lonelyplanet.co.uk

This title was commissioned in Lonely Planet's London office and produced by: **Commissioning Editor** Sally Schafer **Coordinating Editors** Victoria Harrison, Margedd Heliosz **Coordinating Cartographer** Helen Rowley **Layout Designer** Indra Kilfoyle **Cartographers** Emma McNicol, Jack Gavran **Managing Cartographer** Mark Griffiths **Cover Designer** Brendan Dempsey **Project Manager** Rachel Imeson **Mapping Development** Paul Piaia **Desktop Publishing Support** Mark Germanchis **Thanks to** Adriana Mammarella, Celia Wood, Jennifer Garrett, Sally Darmody, Stephanie Pearson, Wayne Murphy

Photographs by Greg Elms/Lonely Planet Images except for the following: p5, p57, p61 Hannah Levy/Lonely Planet Images; p36 (top) Damien Simonis/Lonely Planet Images; p36 (bottom) Robert Harding Picture Library Ltd/Alamy. **Cover photograph** Santiago Calatrava, Stephan Liewehr/age fotostock. All images are copyright of the photographers unless otherwise indicated. Many of the images in this guide are available for licensing from Lonely Planet Images: www.lonelyplanetimages.com.

ISBN 174 104 655 6

Printed through Colorcraft Ltd, Hong Kong. Printed in China

Acknowledgment Metrovalencia Zonal Map © Metrovalencia 2005

Contents

From the Publisher

THE AUTHOR
Miles Roddis

Miles found writing about a city he's called home for nearly 15 years and sharing its secrets enormously satisfying. Of the more than 25 Lonely Planet titles that he's written or contributed to, this is the first where he can truly say, hand on paunch, he's dined in nearly every restaurant that features and drunk in just about every bar.

Special thanks to Ingrid, who knows as much as me about Valencia and corrected some of my waywardness. Thank you to José Díez and Miguel Lorente for the lowdown on the club scene and Lisa Gingles for fashion and shopping pointers. So many keen diners shared with me their favourite restaurants: Steve Anderson, Juan Sánchez, Carla and Peter Taylor, María Vicente, Raquel Ortiz, Pau Marquez, Robert Dean and the Wednesday-morning coffee ladies. *Muchas gracias* too to Elena Gala of Valencia 2007, and María Jover and Dani Arnal at the Calle Paz tourist office for their cheerful enthusiasm. Lastly, a glass raised to fellow writers Jason Webster and Derek Workman, with whom I've shared many a dinner and congenial *copa*.

LONELY PLANET AUTHORS
Why is our travel information the best in the world? It's simple: our authors are independent, dedicated travellers. They don't research using just the Internet or phone, and they don't take freebies in exchange for positive coverage. They travel widely, to all the popular spots and off the beaten track. They personally visit thousands of hotels, restaurants, cafés, bars, galleries, palaces, museums and more – and they take pride in getting all the details right, and telling it how it is. For more, see the authors section on **www.lonelyplanet.com**.

PHOTOGRAPHER
Greg Elms

Greg Elms has been a contributor to Lonely Planet for over 15 years, and has completed numerous commissions in that time, including five books in the World Food series – Mexico, Turkey, France, India and China. The city guides in particular provide a chaotic mix of search-and-shoot photography in often less-than-ideal conditions. In Valencia it rained almost every day of the shoot – in a city where it supposedly never rains. Fortunately many of the 140 locations covered were indoors – and frequent plates of fresh local mussels helped fuel the journey. Greg was ably assisted in navigating Valencia's labyrinthine Centro Historico by the friendly folk at Valencia Tourism.

SEND US YOUR FEEDBACK
We love to hear from travellers – your comments keep us on our toes and help make our books better. Our well-travelled team reads every word on what you loved or loathed about this book. Although we cannot reply individually to postal submissions, we always guarantee that your feedback goes straight to the appropriate authors, in time for the next edition – and the most useful submissions are rewarded with a free book. To send us your updates – and find out about Lonely Planet events, newsletters and travel news – visit our award-winning website: **www.lonelyplanet.com/feedback**.

Note: We may edit, reproduce and incorporate your comments in Lonely Planet products such as guidebooks, websites and digital products, so let us know if you don't want your comments reproduced or your name acknowledged. For a copy of our privacy policy visit **www.lonelyplanet.com/privacy**.

Introducing Valencia

Let's put Valencia first, for once. So often compared in the same breath to the capital, Madrid, or Catalan Barcelona, this lovely city nowadays speaks for itself – yet always with a sideways glance at what its big sisters are up to and an occasional thumb of the nose in their direction.

For an increasing number of visitors, though, Spain's third-largest city is their first choice for a short break. They come to shop in the designer emporia and feisty boutiques, to stroll the historic quarter and to visit the architecturally stunning Ciudad de las Artes y las Ciencias complex, the Instituto Valenciano de Arte Moderno (IVAM) – one of Spain's best contemporary art galleries – and the splendours of the Museo de Bellas Artes. Most recently, the old port has been comprehensively spruced up and made more accessible in anticipation of Valencia's hosting the 2007 America's Cup yacht races.

Valencia's very much a party town too. Las Fallas, Europe's wildest street party, celebrated in mid-March, sets the tone, but every weekend the nightlife throbs until well beyond dawn. For nine months of the year you can sprawl on the beach; 'we don't do clouds' was a recent slogan, promoting a city that has more than 300 cloudless days each year and more than 3km of broad sand. At the heart of the *huerta* – a fertile agricultural plain rich in citrus groves – the Big Orange offers the freshest fruit and vegetables. And paella, nowadays truly international, first simmered over a wood fire here in Valencia...

Lashings of luminous lace and squillions of sequins make sweet señoritas smile at Las Fallas

Neighbourhoods

Valencia city, flat as a pancake, seriously sprawls, its outer suburbs each year nibbling away more of the shrinking *huerta* (the region's fertile coastal plain). But the Valencia that matters to visitors is a wonderfully compact nucleus, easily explored on foot. The **Centro Histórico** is an oval area bounded by the former course of the Río Turia, long ago diverted, and the sickle-shaped inner ring road of Calles Colón, Xàtiva and Guillem de Castro. These trace the walls of the old city, demolished in 1865 as a job-creation project (you can 'see' the walls by hopping on bus 5, which skirts the limits). Within these confines are three major squares: **Plaza del Ayuntamiento**, **Plaza de la Reina** (also known as Plaza de Zaragoza) and **Plaza de la Virgen**.

OFF THE BEATEN TRACK
Overly baroque-bashed or mauled by too much Modernista? Then beat a hasty retreat to the calm greenhouse at the Jardín Botánico (p28) or the more intimate Jardín de Monforte (p28).

In the Centro Histórico's northwest quadrant, bounded by Calles Caballeros, Serranos and Guillem de Castro, lies the **Barrio del Carmen** (El Carmé), the city's oldest area, rich in bars and restaurants.

The old city walls were razed in the 19th century for the expansion of the city. The new area is known as **L'Eixample** (El Ensanche in Spanish, 'The Extension'). Here, east of Gran Vía Marqués del Turia, you'll find grand bourgeois apartments, designer shops and the wonderful Modernista Mercado de Colón, a vast one-time market building. Abutting L'Eixample, south of Avenida Antic Regne de Valencia, is the traditionally working-class district of **Russafa**, nowadays enriched by recent immigrants and enticing restaurants and bars.

North of the former river bed, wide Avenida Blasco Ibañez extends eastwards to the coast, the popular district of **Cabanyal**, and the beach and restaurant areas of **Las Arenas** and **La Malvarrosa**. Just to their south, the bustling commercial port lies beyond the rejuvenated **old port**, heart of America's Cup action.

STREET NAMES & ADDRESSES
Street signs, increasingly, are only in Valenciano. Our maps use the Spanish version, which is the one everyone understands if you ask directions and the form most frequently used by hotels and restaurants. On the few occasions where forms differ radically, the Valenciano version is shown in brackets – for example Calle Alta (Dalt).

You may come across an address ending in s/n. It stands for *sin número* (without number), and indicates that a place has no street number.

Itineraries

Valencia merits a good week of your life but few visitors can afford such indulgence. Here are suggestions for three full days of activity.

Day One

The **Ciudad de las Artes y las Ciencias** (p10) takes a full day to explore. The Oceanogràfic is a must; an IMAX film at the Hemisfèric rests weary feet. If you're game for more, head into town for the **Palacio del Marqués de Dos Aguas** (p18) and, within it, the Museo Nacional de Cerámica.

Day Two

Begin by browsing the **Mercado Central** (p14), then cross the road to explore former silk exchange **La Lonja** (p13). Visit the cathedral and basilica of **Nuestra Señora de los Desamparados** (p8). After a coffee in the square, take in the multimedia show at **Cripta de la Cárcel de San Vicente Mártir** (p22). The afternoon is for museums: the **Museo de Bellas Artes** (p11) and **Instituto Valenciano de Arte Moderno** (IVAM; p12).

Day Three

Take the bus or high-speed tram for a seaside morning, exploring the **old port** (p16), walking the splendid *paseo marítimo* (seafront promenade), and perhaps relaxing on the beach and enjoying a swim. For lunch, order a paella at one of the Las Arenas beach side restaurants.

In the afternoon, grab a taxi and visit the **Museo de Historia de Valencia** (p15) at the city's western extremity. Time it right and you can climb the small hillock in adjacent **Parque de la Cabecera** (p28) to watch the sun set over town.

WORST OF VALENCIA
- Streets slick with dog turds
- Oh the noise! – see p67
- Cars parked illegally and with impunity (over 600,000 parking tickets were slapped on windscreens in 2004; fewer than 90,000 drivers paid up)

But are they fresh? Hungry diners watch the people parading through Oceanogràfic's tunnel

Highlights

PLAZA DE LA VIRGEN (2, D3)

Pedestrianised Plaza de la Virgen sits on what was once the forum of Roman Valencia. Nowadays, it's a pleasant spot for a lingering drink on one of the square's terraces, surrounded by fine buildings.

INFORMATION

- € cathedral incl audioguide €3/2.10; bell tower €1.20/0.60
- ☾ cathedral 7am-1pm & 4.30-8.30pm; bell tower 10am-1pm & 4.30-8pm Mon-Sat, 10am-1pm & 5-6.30pm Sun; Nuestra Señora de los Desamparados 7am-2pm & 4-9pm
- 🚌 4, 5B, 6, 8, 9, 11, 16, 28, 36, 70, 71
- ✕ Seu-Xerea (p52)

The cathedral backdrop at Plaza de la Virgen

You may find it crowded but numbers are nothing compared to those on the morning of the second Sunday in May. Then, the Virgin makes the journey, all of 200m but lasting over 20 minutes, from her basilica and in through the cathedral's baroque doors, as passionate crowds surge to touch her robes. On 17 and 18 March, over 20,000 *falleros* and *falleras* (male and female fiesta participants) join a procession, bearing bouquets and huge mounted displays of flowers as offerings to the Virgin Mary, who gives her name to the square.

The handsome reclining figure in the square's central fountain represents the Río Turia, while the eight maidens with their gushing pots are symbolic of the main irrigation canals flowing from the river.

The **cathedral** (enter from Plaza de la Reina) was erected on the site of Valencia's main mosque shortly after the city was reconquered from the Moors. Added to and modified over the centuries, it's a microcosm of Valencia's architectural history. The **Puerta del Palau** is purest Romanesque. The dome, tower and **Puerta de los Apóstoles**, which is the venue every Thursday at noon for the Tribunal de las Aguas

Detail of the cathedral's intricate doors

Staying cool Turia fountain style

(Water Court; p30), are Gothic; the presbytery and main entrance on Plaza de la Reina are baroque; and there are a couple of Renaissance chapels inside.

In the flamboyant Gothic **Capilla del Santo Cáliz**, to the right of the main entrance, is what's claimed to be the **Holy Grail**, the chalice from which Christ sipped during the Last Supper and one of a dozen or more rival claimants. A door leads to the cathedral **museum** with its rich collection of vestments and statuary. The next chapel along, **La Capilla de San Francisco de Borja**, has a pair of particularly sensitive Goyas. Looking up, see the way the suffused light streams through the translucent alabaster windows of the tower above the main altar.

For great 360-degree city and skyline views, turn left as you enter the cathedral and clamber up the 207 spiralling steps of the octagonal **Miguelete bell tower**.

Above the altar of the basilica of **Nuestra Señora de los Desamparados**, begun in 1652, is an ornate, much venerated statue of the Virgin, patron of the city. If you arrive after hours, peer in through the grilles on the southern, cathedral side, and push your nose against its bars, worn smooth over the years by tens of thousands of supplicants.

Opposite the basilica is the handsome 15th-century Gothic – and much amended – **Palau de la Generalitat** (p26).

DON'T MISS
- The view from the top of the Miguelete bell tower
- A café terrace drink stop
- The ornate Virgen de los Desamparados statue

CIUDAD DE LAS ARTES Y LAS CIENCIAS (3, E4)

The aesthetically stunning **Ciudad de las Artes y las Ciencias** (City of Arts & Sciences) occupies a huge 350,000-sq-metre swath of the former Turia river bed. Bursting from what was previously rank, untended marshland, it pulls in well over four million visitors annually – a figure outstripped in Spain only by Madrid's Prado museum. It's mostly the work of internationally renowned local architect Santiago Calatrava (see p26).

The highlight, especially if you have young children, is the **Oceanogràfic**, in whose aquariums sloshes sufficient water to fill 15 Olympic-size swimming pools. Unlike the rest of the complex, it was designed by the prominent Spanish-American architect Félix Candela, who died in 1997 before he could see the completion of his daring creation. This watery world, the largest of its kind in Europe, has, among much else, polar zones, a dolphinarium, a Red Sea aquarium, a Mediterranean seascape and a couple of underwater tunnels – one 70m long, where schools of fish, including sharks, giant eels and rays, swim all around you.

> **DON'T MISS**
> • Fairy penguins in the Oceanogràfic
> • The Oceanogràfic's dolphin show
> • The illuminated Ciudad de las Artes y las Ciencias viewed after dark from Puente Monteolivete
> • The Science Museum's Life & the Genome section

The spiky exterior of the **Museo de las Ciencias Príncipe Felipe** recalls the skeleton of a giant whale. Each section of this interactive science museum has an explanatory English pamphlet. The innards aren't as exciting as the structure itself but there are still plenty of touchy-feely things for children and machines and displays to arouse even the most unscientific of adults.

The **Hemisfèric** broods like a huge, heavy-lidded eye over the shallow lake around it. It's at once planetarium, IMAX cinema and laser show. You can listen to your soundtrack in four languages, including English.

The **Palau de les Arts Reina Sofia**, a multifunctional arts complex with four auditoriums, is destined for its first public performances in autumn 2006. For more details, see p25.

INFORMATION

☎ reservations 902 100031
💻 www.cac.es
✉ Autovia a El Saler
€ Oceanogràfic €21.20/16; Museo de las Ciencias Príncipe Felipe €7.20/5.60; Hemisfèric €7.20/5.60; combination tickets available
☽ 10am-6pm Sun-Fri, 10am-8pm Sat mid-Sep–mid-Jun, 10am-8pm mid-Jun–mid-Sep
🚌 13, 14, 15, 19, 35, 40, 95
🅿 per hr €1.60
♿ good
🍴 Restaurante Submarino (p57) & on-site snack bars

Is is a beetle? No, it's the famed Hemisfèric

MUSEO DE BELLAS ARTES (2, E2)

Valencia's Fine Arts Museum ranks among Spain's best. Once a fusty, ill-lit place, it's now, following extensive renovations, bright, spacious and worthy of its splendid collection. The ground floor houses mainly religious art, confiscated in 1837 (like the basis of so many Spanish museum collections) when the state seized ecclesiastical properties. Highlights include several magnificent late medieval altarpieces (especially the *Retablo del Fray Bonifacio Ferrer*) and, out of kilter with all the rest, the grotesque features of the participants in a triptych of the Passion of Christ by a follower of Hieronymus Bosch. On the 1st floor are works by the greats such as El Greco, Murillo, Morales, Goya and Velázquez. The museum is also well endowed with canvases from Valencia's first golden age of painting, with works by internationally recognised artists such as Ribera, Ribalta and Juan de Juanes. On this floor too is the magnificent Roman *Mosaic of the Nine Muses*. Up on the 2nd floor are galleries featuring the Valencian impressionist school and its leading exponents, Sorolla and Pinazo.

INFORMATION

☎ 96 360 57 93
🖳 www.cult.gva.es/mbav in Spanish
✉ Calle San Pío V 9
€ free
🕙 10am-8pm Tue-Sun
🚍 1, 5B, 6, 8, 26, 79, 95
♿ fair
🍴 excellent on-site café

DON'T MISS

• Velázquez' self-portrait
• The *Mosaic of the Nine Muses*
• Francisco Ribalta's *San Francisco abrazado al crucificado*

Given such tranquil surroundings as the lush green forecourt, consider lingering for lunch or resting your feet awhile in the museum's congenial café.

INSTITUTO VALENCIANO DE ARTE MODERNO (2, B2)

IVAM (*ee*-bam) is one of Europe's finest museums of contemporary art. Permanent elements include a whole gallery of spiky, abstract creations in metal by Catalan sculptor Julio González, and other artists of his era, another area devoted to the late-19th-century Valencian artist Ignacio Pinazo, and two galleries displaying a selection from the museum's superb collection of photography from early black-and-white prints to modern times. Most visitors come to enjoy the museum's temporary exhibitions, which are hugely varied and of a consistently high standard.

Mixing the strictly contemporary with the past, there's a hefty length of the old city wall in a gallery beneath the museum that's reserved for temporary exhibitions. Also well worth a visit is IVAM's bookshop, which carries much more than books (you'll find many titles in English) and is a great source of stylish gifts for the folks back home.

At the time of writing, the museum was in the throes of a major expansion, designed by renowned Japanese architects Kazuyo Sejima and Ryue Nishizawa.

INFORMATION

☎ 96 386 30 00
🖳 www.ivam.es
✉ Calle Guillem de Castro 118
€ €2/1
🕙 10am-8pm Tue-Sun Oct-May,
   10am-10pm Tue-Sun Jun-Sep
ℹ free guided tours in Spanish at noon
   Sat, 11am & 12.30pm Sun Sep-Jul
🚌 5, 28, 80, 95
♿ excellent
🍴 La Sucursal (p48)

DON'T MISS
- The well-endowed bookshop
- Julio Gonzalez' *Femme au Miroir*
- Pinazo's *After Mass in Godella*

Don't forget to look up ... there are lots of quirky rooftop sculptures

LA LONJA (2, C4)

Fifteenth-century Gothic La Lonja was founded in 1498 as an early Valencian commodity exchange and meeting place for the merchant classes. Now listed as a Unesco World Heritage site, the sweeping lines

Sticks of barley sugar or helicoidal columns – a fascinating feat of La Lonja's architecture

of La Lonja are the perfect antidote if you're suffering from a twinge of indigestion at the rich baroque all around town. The rib-vaulted ceiling of the main colonnaded hall is supported by what experts refer to as helicoidal columns wonderful, slim, twisted pillars curling up high like sticks of barley sugar. They invite architectural metaphor: fashioned to resemble skeins of silk, some aver, crafted to suggest the ropes and hawsers of the merchant ships that brought and exported the city's wealth, say others. The Consulado del Mar (which was closed for renovations at the time of writing) is a side room that was once a separate building and has a stunning *artesonado* (moulded ceiling).

Entry is free at the moment, although once the renovations are completed, there may be a charge for La Lonja. Then, the Sunday morning stamp and coin collectors, long banished to the pavement outside, may once again be allowed in to exchange and trade, sustaining in their modest, part-time way the building's original function.

INFORMATION

✉ Plaza del Mercado
€ free
☽ 10am-2pm & 4.30-8.30pm Tue-Sat, 10am-3pm Sun
🚌 7, 27, 28, 81
✕ Tasca Ángel (p53)

DON'T MISS

- The elaborate coffered ceiling of the Consulado del Mar
- The vibrant, stunted carvings that climb the ribs of the main entrance
- The obscene carvings that pop up here and there, and which we'll leave for you to discover!

MERCADO CENTRAL (2, C4)

Facing the Gothic splendour of La Lonja across Plaza del Mercado, Valencia's Modernista central market more than holds its own. Completed in 1928, it's a swirl of smells, movement and colour. There are still over 900 active stalls despite ever-keener competition from supermarkets.

INFORMATION

⊠ Plaza del Mercado
🕑 7.30am-2.30pm Mon-Sat
🚍 7, 27, 28, 81
♿ fair
🍴 Cardamom (p50)

The fish market, in an annexe on its northern side, has everything from eels, still slithering, to swordfish. Most colourful of all are the stalls brimming with shellfish. Savour too the pair of counters in one corner specialising in sheep's heads, lungs and other offal.

Take in too the structure: the way the light pours in (pity about the netting to protect you from pigeon droppings), the glowing coloured glass and the mosaics on the façade.

Outside, look up at the cockatoo (or could it be budgie?), green with verdigris, above the roof. According to legend, desperate fathers from the poverty-stricken villages of inland Aragón would bring to the big city a son the family could no longer afford to feed. 'Look at that odd bird up there', the father would say. Then, as the child gazed upwards, Dad would slip away into the crowd, and the boy, a de facto orphan, would find work as a market porter or day labourer – if luck was on his side.

DON'T MISS

- The fish market
- The giant paella pans on sale outside the main entrance
- The spice sellers' kaleidoscope of colours

MUSEO DE HISTORIA DE VALENCIA

Above the equally as new river-bed Parque de Cabecera, this new museum occupies a vast, cathedral-like glazed-brick building that was once a municipal water cistern. Hands-on and very visual with plenty of film

The spectacular former municipal water cistern

and video, it's great fun. It plots more than 2000 years of the city's history. At the hugely interactive Time Machine, you can twirl the steering wheel and call up themes such as local fiestas or the story of the city walls across the centuries. There's an optional English soundtrack to the engaging large screen video mini-dramas, though you'll find the acting and language toe-curlingly stilted at times. To stay in historical sequence, follow the numbered panels – not always easy and you'll need to cast around – finishing at the small, simulated cinema that shows Valencia from the earliest days of the film industry. Arm yourself with the museum's informative English-language folder, which you return as you leave.

INFORMATION

☎ 96 370 11 05
🖳 www.valencia.es/mhv
✉ Calle Valencia
€ €2/1
🕑 9.15am-2pm & 5.30-9pm Tue-Sat, 9.15am-2pm Sun Apr-Sep, 9.15am-2pm & 4.30-8pm Tue-Sat, 9.15am-2pm Sun Oct-Mar
🚌 3, 7, 17, 20, 29, 70, 81, 95
Ⓜ Nou d'Octubre
♿ good

DON'T MISS

- Whirling back across the centuries in the Time Machine
- The cinema's scratchy early clips of Valencia before the motorcar ruled the streets
- Roman mural from the 2nd-century
- The fantastical gargoyle from the Torres de Serranos (panel 22)

Dressing 18th-century-Valencian style

PORT, LAS ARENAS & LA MALVARROSA (MAP 4)

While it's business and bustle as usual in Valencia's outer, commercial port, the inner harbour has undergone a massive change in preparation for the 2007 America's Cup sailing jamboree. Old stores and warehouses

Seemingly perfect symmetry of the former port building

have been demolished. The best of them, repainted and recycled as temporary art galleries, have been kept, together with the original, Italianate port building and its handsome clock tower. A freshly dug canal gives competitors easy access to the open sea, and bright, glass cubes, one for each team, shimmer around the harbour rim. The fishing boats, turfed out from their traditional landing area and wholesale market, are now on the far south side. Drop by around 5pm and you can wander the jetty and inspect the day's catch.

INFORMATION

- 🚌 1, 2, 19, 20, 21, in summer 22 & 23
- 🚋 Eugenia Viñes
- ♿ fair
- 🍴 Lonja del Pescado Frito (p58)

North of the port, the **Paseo Marítimo**, an elegant promenade, extends for over 3km beside the broad beaches of **Las Arenas** (The Sands) and **La Malvarrosa**, groomed daily in summer and a magnificent playground at the seaside limit of this busy city.

DON'T MISS

- Sensing the contrast between the ultramodern America's Cup port and what's been kept of the old harbour
- A lunchtime paella overlooking the beach
- Bouncing on the stretchy, pyramid-shaped beach climbing frames

TORRES DE SERRANOS (2, C2)

Once the main exit to Barcelona and the north, the well-preserved 14th-century Torres de Serranos, freshly scrubbed and softly illuminated at night, overlook the bed of Río Turia. For a full 300 years, the towers' lower rooms also served as a lock-up for wealthier prisoners.

It's worth climbing the 132 steps to the battlements for an impressive panoramic view of the old quarter with less input than the longer slog up the stairs of the Miguelete bell tower (p9). From here, in the lead up to Las Fallas, the *fallera mayor* (the 'queen' of that year's festivities) proclaims the *crida* (an invitation to participate) to the thousands of chanting *falleros* below, followed by the first of the season's spectacular firework displays.

See p27 for details of the Torres de Quart, which are as imposing though less embellished. They and

INFORMATION

☎ 96 391 90 70
✉ Plaza de los Fueros
€ €2/1
🕓 10am-2pm & 4.30-8.30pm Tue-Sat, 10am-3pm Sun
🚌 2, 5, 5B, 6, 8, 11, 16, 80, 95
🍴 Mattilde (p48)

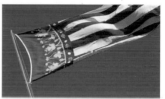

Flying the flag at Torres de Serranos

Torres de Serranos are all that remain intact of the old Christian-era city walls, demolished in the mid-19th century as the city expanded.

HELLO SOLDIER

Soldiers guarding the city's northern exit were billeted above the main gate. To prevent them ever plotting revolt and turning their guns on the town, the canny burghers made their quarters open, looking down on the populace – and allowing the populace to keep an eye on their protectors, just in case...

PALACIO DEL MARQUÉS DE DOS AGUAS (2, D4)

You come here for two reasons: the palace itself and the **Museo Nacional de Cerámica** within.

The 15th-century palace was first modified in the mid-18th century. From this time too dates the alabaster main doorway, where whorls of vegetation and twists of water surround a serene Virgin and Child, the whole propped up by a very muscly pair of Herculean caryatids. It was designed by a local sculptor, Hipólito Rovira, who later went insane and committed suicide. With only a pinch of imagination, you can see the makings of madness in this wonderfully extravagant piece of rococo excess. Most of the building, with its sumptuous marble and fabric wall coverings, dates from the mid-19th century. The ground and 1st floors, with the gilded excess of its ballroom and Red Salon, are furnished in period style.

The 2nd floor presents a sweeping history of ceramics from Roman times to the present day. There's ample representation from the renowned local production centres of Manises and Paterna to the west of town. Their kilns have been fired up ever since Arab times and are still major producers of ceramics today.

INFORMATION

- ☎ 96 351 63 92
- ✉ Calle Poeta Querol 2
- € €2.40/free (free Sat afternoon & Sun)
- ◷ 10am-2pm & 4-8pm Tue-Sat, 10am-2pm Sun
- ▣ 4, 6, 8, 26, 31
- ♿ fair
- ✕ Burdeos in Love (p49)

DON'T MISS

- Picasso's four plates
- The top-floor Valencian kitchen
- The marques's gilded carriage

ESTACIÓN DEL NORTE (2, C6)

It took a full 11 years to construct Valencia's main train station, from the laying of the first stone in 1906 to its spectacular inauguration in 1917. Like many of the great terminals of Europe, it was built to impress – to implant in the newly arrived visitor a positive first impression of the city.

The exterior of this U-shaped structure seems a cross between a mock castle and a rich, creamy wedding cake garnished with oranges. It's a gorgeous example of Valencian Modernismo, rich in decorative touches that enhance what's in essence a functional place for mass transportation. Granted, much of the decoration nowadays seems a touch clichéd. But it's lovely for all that, even though the weary themes make some contemporary Valencianos squirm.

Illustrative of Valencia's industry and the *huerta* its surrounding market garden, the ceramic mosaics depict cheery peasant women in traditional costume with naked, frolicking children at their skirts, baskets brimming with fruit, bouquets of roses and friezes of oranges. The main hall is a delight of stained wood and *trencadí,* the slivers-of-broken-tile mosaic style associated historically with Gaudí and today with Santiago Calatrava, Valencia's own son (see p26). Estación del Norte is not an ordinary train station.

INFORMATION

✉ Calle Xàtiva 24

Ⓜ Xàtiva, Bailén

♿ excellent

🍴 FrescCo (p51)

Waiting for trains isn't always this stylish

THANKS FOR YOUR GOOD WISHES

In the main hall of the station, the wording 'Bon voyage' is picked out in gold leaf in major languages, including Arabic and Chinese. 'Pleasant journey', it quaintly wishes the Anglophone traveller...

AMERICA'S CUP 2007

In 2007 the **America's Cup yacht races** (www.americascup.com) return to Europe for the first time since the inaugural competition in 1851. Why so long? Because 2003 was the first time a European boat finally triumphed when, in Auckland, New Zealand, the Swiss yacht *Alinghi* ruled the waves. But why Valencia? Because the rules (and yachties love rules and regulations) determine that races must take place at sea and landlocked Switzerland, as reigning champ and host, can't muster a drop.

The Swiss chose Valencia, where wind offshore is all but guaranteed yet rarely blustery; most days, the *garbí*, a warm southeasterly wind, blows at a steady 10 to 15 knots. With precisely 3.8 days of coastal fog each year, the chances of a maritime whiteout are negligible. Spectators, too, benefit; racing takes place only 15 minutes' sailing time from the port, beating up and down the coast off the beaches and promenades of Las Arenas and La Malvarrosa.

In 1851 the schooner *America* (hence the apostrophe in America's Cup) defeated 15 British yachts off the Isle of Wight to win a prize of 100 guineas and a handsome trophy. Since then, the cup's been competed for on 31 occasions. US yachts have won a massive 27 of the subsequent races with New Zealand triumphing twice, Australia once – then, improbably and latterly, Switzerland. (Not that you'll find too many Swiss sailors in the crew – only five out of a team of 35, in fact. *Alinghi,* like most other teams, has a truly international cast, including eight New Zealanders.)

Ever since September 2004, the 12 potential challengers from nine countries and five continents have been battling it out in 13 'Acts'. These regattas lead up to the Louis Vuitton Cup (April to June 2007), whose winner has the privilege of taking on *Alinghi* in single combat, as three years of action culminate in the America's Cup races themselves (late June to July 2007).

Local and central government investment in the event is estimated at around €400 million. Around the inner harbour, the Balcón al Mar (Balcony to the Sea) occupies 425,000 sq metres of land reclaimed from the sea and recycled from dilapidated port buildings. There's a competitors' village with shops, restaurants and cafés and, open to the general public, the Foredeck, a 107,000-sq-metre cultural and leisure facility.

Elsewhere, the impetus of the Cup has hastened the expansion of the metro to the airport, which is getting a much-needed second runway. New hotels burgeon and a one-way five-lane highway links port and downtown, replacing the previous traffic-clogged artery, as, impelled by the wind of the America's Cup, Valencia sails deeper into the 21st century.

Sights & Activities

MUSEUMS & GALLERIES

Baños del Almirante (2, D3)
These Arab-style baths, built in 1313 shortly after the Reconquest, functioned continuously as public bathing facilities until 1959. There's an excellent audio-visual presentation with optional English commentary, and guided visits every half hour.
☎ 60 527 57 84 ✉ Calle Baños del Almirante 3-5 € free ☉ 10am-2pm & 6-8pm Tue-Sat, 10am-2pm Sun 🚍 2, 5, 16, 28, 80

Casa de las Rocas (2, C2)
Behind tall doors rest the giant carts that are wheeled out just once a year for Valencia's Corpus Christi festival in June and pulled to the Plaza de la Virgen. Their paintwork is darkened with age; the earliest dates back to the 16th century.
☎ 96 392 23 26 ✉ Calle de las Rocas 3 € €2/1 ☉ 10am-2pm Mon-Fri 🚍 2, 5, 6, 80, 95 ♿ good

No wonder he was inspired— Blasco Ibañez' summer home

Corpus Christi gilded carriage

Casa-Museo Blasco Ibañez (4, A1)
The summer residence of Blasco Ibañez, Valencia's most famous literary son and author of, among many other works, *The Four Horsemen of the Apocalypse*, houses many of his personal belongings and furniture of the period.
☎ 96 352 54 78 ✉ Calle Isabel de Villena s/n € €2/1 ☉ 10am-2pm & 4.30-8.30pm Tue-Sat, 10am-3pm Sun 🚍 1, 2, 19, 31, 32 ♿ fair

Casa-Museo Concha Piquer (3, C1)
Fêted throughout Spain and the Americas, Concha Piquer was, until well into the 1950s, the country's most famous popular singer. She belts out some of her most popular numbers as background to the video of her life.
☎ 96 348 56 58 ✉ Calle Ruaya 23 € €2/1 ☉ 10am-2pm & 4.30-8.30pm Tue-Sat, 10am-3pm Sun 🚍 6, 16, 26, 36 🚊 Sagunt ♿ good

Casa-Museo de la Semana Santa Marinera (4, A3)
This museum displays the rich costumes, vestments, floats and regalia brought into play during the elaborate Semana Santa (Easter Week) processions that wind around the maritime district of Cabanyal.
☎ 96 352 54 78 ✉ Calle Rosario 1 € €2/1 ☉ 10am-2pm & 4.30-8.30pm Mon-Sat, 10am-3pm Sun 🚍 32 🚊 Les Arenas ♿ fair

Casa-Museo José Benlliure (2, C2)

This lovely 19th-century bourgeois villa was the home of Valencian artist, José Benlliure (1855–1937). Furnished in period style, it's also a gallery dedicated to Benlliure and to his contemporaries. Beyond the mature garden at the rear is his agreeably cluttered studio and library.

☎ 96 391 16 62 ⊠ Calle Blanquerías 23 € €2/1 ☼ core hours 9.15am-2pm & 5.30-8pm Tue-Sun, 9.30am-2pm Sun 🚌 2, 5, 26, 80, 95 ♿ excellent

Cripta de la Cárcel de San Vicente Mártir (2, D3)

Reputedly a prison for the 4th-century martyr San Vicente, the city's patron saint, the much damaged crypt's interest lies in its excellent 25-minute multimedia show recounting Valencia's history, and the saint's life and details of his particularly gory death. Phone or call by the Museo de la Ciudad, opposite, to reserve.

☎ 96 394 14 17 ⊠ Plaza del Arzobispo s/n € €2/1

☼ 9.30am-2pm & 5.30-8pm Tue-Sat, 9.30am-2pm Sun 🚌 2, 8, 29, 80, 95 ♿ excellent

Galería del Tossal (2, C3)

Step underground into this small gallery, within it a sizable hunk of Valencia's Arab wall. It's a venue for temporary exhibitions illustrating the city's history and archaeology.

☎ 96 398 18 03 ⊠ Plaza del Tossal € €2/1 ☼ 9.30am-2pm & 5-8pm Tue-Sat, 9.30am-2pm Sun 🚌 5B, 7, 81

Museo de Ciencias Naturales (2, E2)

Within the Jardines del Real, this relatively small natural-science museum has some spectacular local and international shells and fossils, including the skeleton of a huge megathere, a prehistoric beast to rival the dinosaur.

☎ 96 352 54 78, ext 4313 ⊠ Jardines del Real, Calle San Pío V s/n € €2/1 ☼ 9.30am-2pm & 4.30-8pm Tue-Sat, 10am-8pm Sun 🚌 4, 6, 18, 30, 78 ♿ good

Museo de Prehistoria y de las Culturas de Valencia (2, B2)

This museum's name is a mouthful but it's also known more simply as La Beneficencia. Highlights of the 1st floor, which covers the Palaeolithic period, are the rich finds from the Cueva de Parpalló – tools, jewellery, human and animal bones and, important for archaeologists if unexciting for everyone else, over 5000 fragments of limestone bearing incisions and traces of paint. On the 2nd floor, Roman and Iberian artefacts include the Guerrero de Moixent, a dinky 4th-century-BC miniature plumed warrior on horseback.

☎ 96 388 35 65 ⊠ Calle Corona 36 € free ☼ 10am-9pm 🚌 5, 28, 80, 95

Museo del Arroz (4, A3)

This early-20th-century mill husked rice from the fertile fields of the Albufera until the mid-1970s. Presenting the history of local rice cultivation from Arab times onwards, its restored machine again clanks and whirrs.

☎ 96 352 54 78, ext 4075 ⊠ Calle Rosario 1-3 € €2/1 ☼ 10am-2pm & 4.30-8.30pm Tue-Sat, 10am-3pm Sun 🚌 1, 2, 19 ♿ fair

Museo del Artista Fallero

This practical museum, run by the guild of *falla* artists, gives a good idea of how *fallas* (giant sculptures erected in the streets during Las Fallas) are constructed by means of models, plenty of examples and a 25-minute audiovisual show.

SAN VICENTE MÁRTIR'S LEFT ARM

In a case beside the ambulatory that runs behind the main altar of the cathedral in Plaza de la Virgen (pp8) lies a withered and much-travelled relic. San Vicente was martyred around 304 and his body dismembered. In 1108 Teudovildo, the then bishop of Valencia, packed the arm in his baggage for protection as he set out on a pilgrimage for Jerusalem. But before reaching the Holy Land the bishop died, in Bari on Italy's Adriatic coast. The arm spent several centuries in a convent in Venice and was finally returned to Valencia in 1970 by its most recent owner, an Italian from Padua.

☎ 96 347 65 85 ✉ Calle San José Artesano 17 € €1.80/0.60 ☼ 10am-2pm & 4-7pm Mon-Fri, 10am-2pm Sat ☐ 12, 28 Ⓟ ☒ fair

Museo del Patriarca

(2, D4)
This bijou ecclesiastical museum is a must if you're interested in religious art. It's particularly strong on Spanish and Flemish Renaissance painting with several canvases by both Juan de Juanes and Ribalta and a trio of El Grecos. The desiccated alligator above the door is an exhortation to silence; the alligator, unlike the church's more garrulous parishioners, has no tongue.
☎ 96 351 41 76 ✉ Calle de la Nave 1 € €1.20 ☼ 11am-1.30pm ☐ 4, 6 16, 70, 81 ☒ fair

Museo del Trenet

This small museum tells the story of Valencia's former narrow-gauge railway, now superseded by the metro and high-speed tram. Within an old turntable building, it will appeal primarily to train buffs who can read Spanish.
☎ 96 352 54 78 ✉ Parque de Marxalenes € free ☼ 9.15am-2pm & 5.30-9pm Mon-Sat, 9.15am-2pm Sun Apr-Sep, 9.15am-2pm & 4.30-8pm Mon-Sat, 9.15am-2pm Sun Oct-Mar ☐ 6, 16, 26, 36 ☒ Marxalenes ☒ good

Museo Fallero (3, D3)

During Las Fallas, only one of the thousands of *ninots* (near-life-sized figurines that strut and pose at the

Go behind the scenes at Museo del Artista Fallero (left)

base of each *talla*) is saved from the flames each year by popular vote. It's sent here, to rest, forever at peace.
☎ 96 352 54 78, ext 4625 ✉ Plaza Monteolivete s/n € €2/1 ☼ 10am-2pm & 4.30-8.30pm Tue-Sat, 10am-3pm Sun ☐ 13, 15, 19, 35, 95 ☒ fair

Museo Histórico Municipal (2, C5)

Within the Ayuntamiento, this museum is a repository of items important to the city's identity, such as the original Senyera, the regional flag, the sword that Jaime I is reputed to have brandished when defeating the Muslim occupiers and a fascinating 1704 map of Valencia, drafted by Padre Tosca.
☎ 96 352 54 78, ext 1181 ✉ Plaza del Ayuntamiento 1 € free ☼ 9am-2pm Mon-Fri Ⓜ Xàtiva

Museo Taurino (2, D6)

This small museum is full of images of strutting macho men in figure-hugging sequinned suits and funny hats. There's a collection of bullfighting memorabilia and a good 15-minute commentary less video portraying a bull's life on the range up to its tortured death in the ring. You can also visit the adjacent bullring.
☎ 96 388 37 38 ✉ Pasaje Doctor Serra 10 € free ☼ 10am-8pm Tue-Sat, 10am-2pm Sun ☐ 8, 15, 17, 40, 63 Ⓜ Xàtiva

Museo Valenciano de la Ilustración y la Modernidad (Muvim)

(2, B6)
The Museum of the Enlightenment presents the history of ideas and thought through images, dioramas and dialogue. Hour-long tours

Final score one all.
The gorged tear, the sole reminder (p23)

start every half-hour and there's an English audioguide. The English commentary is sometimes muffled and drowned by background music and ambient sound, but just go with the flow of the images.

☎ 96 388 37 47 ✉ Calle Guillem de Castro 8 € free

☯ 10am-2pm & 4-8pm Tue-Sat, 10am-2pm Sun 🚌 5, 11, 71 Ⓜ Àngel Guimerà ♿ fair

Palacio Joan de Valeriola (2, B4)

This 14th-century palace, sensitively restored as a contemporary art gallery, houses temporary exhibitions. Subtle lighting and the extensive use of glass complement perfectly the sweeping Gothic arches of the ground floor and the slender stone windows, polychrome beams and coffered ceilings of its upper storeys.

☎ 96 338 12 15 🖥 www .chirivellasoriano.org ✉ Calle Valeriola 13 € €4 ☯ 10am-2pm & 5-8pm Tue-Sat, 10am-2pm Sun 🚌 7, 60, 81 ♿ good

BEST OF THE BUILDINGS

Almudín (2, D3)

The 15th-century Almudín, which is now used for exhibitions of giant canvases and sculpture, served as the city's granary, storing wheat, brought in from the surrounding countryside.

Writing high up on the interior walls indicates the levels of harvests and where the grain came from.

☎ 96 352 54 78, ext 4521 ✉ Plaza San Luis Beltrán 1 € €2/1 ☯ 10am-2pm & 4.30-8pm Tue-Sat, 10am-3pm Sun 🚌 4, 16, 31, 70, 81 ♿ fair

Central Post Office (2, C5)

Correos, Valencia's resplendent neoclassical main post office, stares across the square at the Town Hall, upstaging it. Even if you don't need any stamps, drop in to admire its spaciousness and superb, recently restored stained-glass ceiling. The winged angels and sculpted train on its roof could perhaps get letters more swiftly to their destination than today's donkey-pace service.

✉ Plaza del Ayuntamiento 24 ☯ 8.30am-8.30pm Mon-Fri, 9.30am-2pm Sat 🚌 4, 6, 10, 19, 36 Ⓜ Xàtiva ♿ fair; access on cnr of Calle Correos

Complexo Deportivo Cultural Petxina (3, A2)

This new sports complex occupies Valencia's former abattoir, with its classical forms of mellow brick. After

It's a ceiling which has left its stamp on Valencia's Central Post Office

PALAU DE LES ARTS REINA SOFIA

This monumental **arts complex** (3, D4; www.lesarts.com), another creation of Santiago Calatrava, broods over the river bed like a giant beetle, its shell shimmering with translucent *trencadís* (slivers-of-broken-tile mosaic). 'The 10th wonder of the world', its artistic director proclaimed with only a measure of hyperbole at the official inauguration in late 2005.

Nine years in construction, the Palau de les Arts Reina Sofia was formally opened in October 2005. The largest opera house in Europe, it's as tall as a 25-storey building. With four auditoriums and seating for 4400, its capacity is exceeded only by the Sydney Opera House. Like Sydney, it ran hopelessly over budget, an initial forecast of €84 million contrasting with a final cost of over €250 million.

The first concert season is planned for October 2006.

languishing, disused, for over a quarter of a century, it again resounds to shouts and squeals of a happier kind. See also p84.

☎ 96 387 04 20 ⊠ Paseo de la Pechina 42 ☽ 8am–10pm Mon–Fri, 8am–7pm Sat, 9am–2pm Sun ☒ 17, 22, 60, 73, 90 Ⓜ Turia ⓖ good

Iglesia de Santa Catalina (2, C4)

This church, badly knocked about in the civil war, is starkly impressive inside. It's dwarfed by the striking 18th-century hexagonal baroque bell tower that's one of the city's best-known landmarks and rivals the cathedral's Miguelete as a symbol of the city.

⊠ Plaza de Santa Catalina € free ☽ 9am–noon & 5–7pm ☒ 7, 27, 28, 81 ⓖ fair

Iglesia del Carmen (2, C2)

The church's massive 17th-century baroque façade is its glory. Within, there's little of interest but for one illuminating detail from recent Spanish history: look for a portly Generalísimo Franco, kneeling, left, among the saints in the

huge wall painting behind the altar.

⊠ Plaza del Carmen ☽ irregular ☒ 2, 5, 5B, 80, 95 ⓖ good

Mercado de Colón (2, F5)

The soaring Mercado de Colón, with its rich ceramic work, outstrips the Mercado Central in its Modernista splendour. No longer a food market, alas, it's now occupied by boutiques, cafés and restaurants.

☎ 96 337 11 01 ⊠ Calle Cirilo Amorós s/n ☽ 8am–midnight ☒ 4, 5, 10, 12, 13 Ⓜ Colón Ⓟ ⓖ good

Palacio de Benicarló (2, C2)

This late-Gothic 15th-century palace was once the family home of the Borjas (known in English as the infamous Borgia popes). Nowadays, it's the seat of the Cortes, parliament of the Valencia region.

⊠ Plaza de San Lorenzo 4 ☒ 2, 5, 27, 29, 80

Palacio de Congresos

The Palacio de Congresos, with its slender columns and shimmering, aluminium,

trowel-shaped roof, takes the breath away. Nicknamed the Pez Varado (Beached Fish), it was designed by British architect Sir Norman Foster.

☎ 96 317 94 00 ☐ www.palcongres-vlc.com ⊠ Avenida de las Cortes Valencianas 60 ☒ 62, 63 Ⓜ Palau de Congressos ⓖ good

On the tiles, Mercado de Colón

Palacio de la Exposición
(3, D2)
Built in 1909 in only 60 days, this jewel of Art Deco and neo-Gothic excess has exuberant stained-glass windows, make-you-blink tilework and a wonderful curlicue wooden staircase that leads nowhere.
☎ 96 398 18 75 ⊠ Calle Galicia 1 € €2/1 ☽ 10am-2pm & 5-8pm Tue-Sat, 10am-2pm Sun 🚍 6, 8, 28, 70, 95

Napoleon's troops left their marks at Torres de Quart (right)

Palau de la Generalitat
(2, C3)
The handsome 15th-century Palau de la Generalitat is the seat of government for the Valencia region. Its symmetry is recent; the renaissance tower – the one facing Plaza de la Virgen – had to wait over 400 years for its perfectly matching partner, which dates back no further than 1951. Tours of the sumptuous interior are by prior arrangement.
☎ 96 386 34 61 ⊠ Calle Caballeros s/n 🚍 2, 5, 6, 36, 80

Puente de la Exposición
(3, D2)
Nicknamed La Peineta – because it resembles the comb that women wear beneath the mantilla – this bridge was Santiago Calatrava's first creation for the city of his birth.
⊠ Paseo de la Alameda 🚍 6, 8, 9, 11, 16, 26, 28, 29, 31, 32, 36, 70, 81 Ⓜ Alameda ♿ excellent

Reales Atarazanas (3, F3)
Nowadays a pleasing venue for temporary exhibitions, this vast building of mellow brick has the dimensions of a cathedral. But its role was strictly secular; just a block back from the port and

SANTIAGO CALATRAVA
International architect Santiago Calatrava, born and educated in Valencia, designs mainly public projects such as bridges, stations, museums and stadiums – creations to be experienced by thousands every single day. You'll recognise his grand-scale structures immediately, his signature as distinctive and easily recognised as the Coca-Cola logo. Technologically, he pushes to the limits what can balance, counter, take and impart stress in concrete, iron and steel. Yet his rearing structures, all sinuous white curves with scarcely a right angle in sight, relate more to things organic: the vast blinking eye of the Hemisfèric; the filigree struts, like veins on a leaf, of the Umbracle; a vast, shaded walkway in the Ciudad de las Artes y las Ciencias.

In Valencia, most of the Ciudad de las Artes y las Ciencias is his design. Drop beneath the Puente de la Exposición to the Alameda metro station. With its soaring struts, it's like stepping into the carcass of a whale. In the Basque country, his Volantín footbridge complements Bilbao's famous Guggenheim Museum nearby. In the USA, he designed the Milwaukee Art Museum on the shores of Lake Michigan and is the architect of the transportation terminal for the new World Trade Center site in New York. And sports fan may recall his eye-catching steel-and-glass dome for the main stadium of the 2004 Athens Olympic games.

constructed in the 14th century, it functioned for centuries as a shipyard.

☎ 96 352 54 78 ✉ Plaza Juan Antonio Benlliure s/n € €2/1 ⊙ 10am-2pm & 4.30-8.30pm Mon-Sat, 10am-3pm Sun 🚌 1, 2, 3, 19, 30 ♿ excellent

Torres de Quart (2, A3)

These twin 15th-century towers, which served for centuries as a prison, were designed to resemble those of the Castel Nuovo in Naples (which at the time belonged to Spain). Up high, you can still see the pockmarks caused by French cannonballs from when Napoleonic troops invaded the city in 1808.

✉ Calle Guillem de Castro 92 🚌 5 Ⓜ Àngel Guimerà

Town Hall (2, C5)

Valencia's handsome Ayuntamiento dominates the square that takes its name. Within, up the ornate marble staircase, are its shimmering Salón de Fiestas and Museo del Ayuntamiento.

✉ Plaza del Ayuntamiento 1 ⊙ 9am-2pm 🚌 4, 6, 10, 19, 36 Ⓜ Xàtiva

PICK OF THE PLAZAS

The plaza, where tight streets emerge into a broader public space, is a feature of every Spanish town. Emblematic Plaza de la Virgen (see p8) is far from the only square that merits a wander.

La Almoina (2, D3)

La Almoina, with substantial foundations dating from Valencia's earliest occupation onwards, is at the heart of the original town. Through the transparent viewing area, set in the pavement, you can look down on the Roman, Arab and Christian remains. Those keen to make a closer acquaintance can drop down and explore the area below.

€ free 🚌 2, 5, 6, 8, 95 ♿ fair

Plaza del Ayuntamiento (2, C5)

If Plaza de la Virgen is the heart of Valencia's spiritual life, here, where town hall and post office face each other in permanent stand-off, is its temporal equivalent. Fountains dance and spurt and precisely 13 flower shops display their floral best from the surrounding *huerta* (market garden), the region's fertile coastal strip.

🚌 4, 6, 10, 19, 36 Ⓜ Xàtiva ♿ excellent

Plaza del Carmen (2, C2)

The massive baroque façade of Iglesia del Carmen (p25) looms over this pleasing, pedestrianised square. Facing it is the less flamboyant but equally impressive frontage of the 18th-century Palacio de Pineda and, within it, Pati Pineda (p49), a great spot for lunch or coffee.

🚌 2, 5, 5B, 80, 95 ♿ excellent

Plaza del Tossal (2, B3)

Around Plaza del Tossal (Square of the Hillock, though you'll scarcely sense any undulation) are some of the finest bars. From it radiate streets – Caballeros, Bolsería, Quart, Alta and Baja – offering even more choice.

🚌 5B, 7, 81

Plaza Redonda (2, C4)

Around this mid-19th-century circular space, constructed on the site of the Mercado Central's former slaughterhouse, stalls sell bits, bobs, buttons and bows, and locally made crafts and ceramics. Lace-makers throw the bobbins on Thursday, from 10am to 1pm. On Sunday morning, the plaza trills with the song of caged birds while, in the adjoining Calle Derechos, mournful puppies and kittens snuggle against their hard-nosed vendors.

🚌 4, 6, 8, 70, 71 ♿ good

Ayuntamiento flower power

PARKS & GARDENS

Jardín Botánico (2, A3)

Established in 1802 and nowadays administered by the University of Valencia, this was Spain's first botanic garden. With mature trees and plants, an extensive cactus garden and a lovely restored 19th-century shade house, it's a tranquil place to relax.

☎ 96 315 68 00 ✉ Calle Quart 80 € €0.60 🕑 10am-dusk Tue-Sun 🚍 5, 7, 81, 95 🚹 good

Jardín de los Hespérides (3, B2)

Beside the Jardín Botánico, this prize-winning modern garden couldn't be more remote in style. Shorter on green space, it has the formality of a classic French garden with cypresses, low banks of herbs and staggered terraces, where tangy citrus trees flourish.

✉ Paseo de la Pechina € free 🕑 10am-8pm Apr-Sep, 10am-6pm Oct-Mar 🚹 fair

Jardín de Monforte (3, D1)

This little haven of tranquillity, where languid Italianate statues pose between clipped knee-high boxwood hedges, is a favourite spot for bridal photos. There's no more pleasant place in town to munch your sandwiches, catch up on the newspaper or grab a quick nap.

✉ Calle Monforte s/n € free 🕑 10.30am-8pm Apr-Sep, to 6pm Oct-Mar 🚍 12, 29, 40, 79, 80 🚹 fair

Jardines del Real (2, E1)

Reaching down to the Jardines del Turia are the Jardines del Real (Royal Gardens), more commonly called Los Viveros. Popular with *valencianos*, this is another lovely spot for a stroll and a drink at one of the several café terraces.

✉ Calle San Pío V s/n € free 🕑 6.30am-9.30pm Apr-Sep, 8.30am-8.30pm Oct-Mar 🚍 1, 26, 32, 79, 81 🚹 good

Jardines del Turia (2, C1)

The former riverbed of the Río Turia is now a 9km-long lung of green – a glorious mix of playing fields, cycling, jogging and walking paths, trees, fountains, lawns and playgrounds, including the ever-patient Gulliver (p30).

€ free

Parque de la Cabecera

Over 1km long, this recently landscaped segment of the river bed has a mini lake, where you can hire swan-shaped pedalos or take a dip. Climb the hillock, for all the world like a Mesopotamian ziggurat, for a great view of the river bed and city.

✉ Paseo de la Pechina € free Ⓜ Nou d'Octubre

FUN THINGS TO DO

Calma (2, C5)

Odd to find a spa-and-beauty centre right in the heart of town, but smart, recently opened Calma has the works – massages from foot to cranium and all zones in-between, showers and baths of all kinds (including the intriguing cromotherapy

Look but don't touch at Jardín Botánico

TRINQUET

Trinquet is the Valencian version of Basque pelota, played with the bare hands, taped to reduce the impact of the small, hard leather ball. It's played over a narrow net, like badminton or tennis. Everything counts — the rear and side walls, even the raked seating where spectators sit and raucously place side bets (it's not rare for quite large wads of euros to change hands).

To see this very Valencian ball game, visit **Bar Trinquet Pelayo** (2, C6; Calle Pelayo 6), near Estación del Norte. Matches begin around 5pm Wednesday to Saturday and admission costs around €5.

'colour bath') and pampering skin treatments.

☎ 902 270007 🖳 www.calma.es ✉ Periodista Azzati 1 🕲 10am-10pm Mon-Sat, 10am 2pm Sun 🚌 4, 6, 17, 19, 36 Ⓜ Xàtiva

Carriage Rides (2, D4)
Hire a horse-drawn carriage in Plaza de la Reina and enjoy clip clopping around the Centro Histórico, lording it over the pedestrians. A 40-minute trip costs €30 for up to five passengers.
✉ Plaza de la Reina 🚌 4, 6, 8, 28, 36

Feria Valencia
Valencia's *feria* (fair) ground is on the city's northern outskirts. The world's 10th largest venue for industrial fairs, it pulls in over a million visitors annually. Themes include antiques, art, DIY, horticulture, cars, even funerary services. Consult the website or any tourist office for topics that might coincide with your visit.
☎ 902 747330 🖳 www.feriavalencia.com ✉ Avenida de las Ferias s/n 🚋 Flra Ⓜ Les Carolines-Fira

Fly a Kite
The seaside breezes are ideal for a little personal kite flying. The seriously kite-committed take over the skies for one long colourful weekend in April, when Valencia celebrates its International Kite Festival with dancing, swirling kites, from jumbos that could almost lift you into space to zippy acrobatic little numbers, scarcely larger than a parrot.

✉ Playas de las Arenas & La Malvarrosa 🚌 1, 2, 19, 32 🚋 Les Arenas, Eugenia Viñes

Golondrinas Transvimar (4, A3)
These small sightseeing boats moor beside renovated Tinglado (warehouse) No 2; look for the giant crane just outside it. You may have to wait a while for your 35-minute chug around the port until the boat's full to the captain's satisfaction.
☎ 96 316 41 77 ✉ Muelle de la Aduana € €4 🕲 9am-sunset 🚌 1, 2, 19, 32

ONLY IN VALENCIA

Cat House (2, B2)
On calle Museo, glance down to knee level opposite No 5. There's a hole for feral cats around which someone has sculpted a miniature house façade with doors, windows and fountain. The original disappeared when the neighbouring building was demolished. Then, one day unannounced, its even more impressive successor arrived.
☎ private fe-line ✉ Calle Museo

There's more than one way to see Valencia

TOMATINA

Buñol? It'll make you see red! On the last or penultimate Wednesday in August (the date varies), an estimated 40,000 people take part in Spain's messiest and most bizarre festival. La Tomatina, creation of Buñol, an otherwise drab industrial town about 40km west of Valencia, is a tomato-throwing orgy.

The festival's origins, though relatively recent, are obscure but who cares? Just before noon on this very red-letter day, truckloads of ripe, squishy tomatoes (over 100 tonnes of them) are tipped out to the waiting crowd and everyone joins in a frenzied, cheerful, anarchic tomato battle, while locals play hoses and throw buckets of water on the seething, increasingly red mass below.

At 1pm an explosion signals the end. Most people come for the day, taking the train from Valencia. If you do take part, put on your oldest clothes and consider goggles or a face mask too. Then again, you could always watch the spectacle in comfort on Canal 9, Valencia's local TV channel...

House of the America's Cup (4, A4)

Put on your headphones, preset to the English commentary, feel the lure of the ocean and follow the history of the America's Cup from the first mid-19th-century challenge in Cowes, UK, to the latest battle of the big boats here in Valencia. Its future is uncertain however: once the last

Find the cat house (p29)

race is run in mid-2007 the House may be demolished. ⊠ Calle Doctor José Dómine € free ⏲ 11am-2pm & 4-8pm ⊜ 1, 2, 3, 19, 30 ♿ good

Tribunal de las Aguas

For over 1000 years, as the bell tolls the 12 strokes of noon, this Water Court sits in judgement outside the Puerta de los Apóstoles at the cathedral (2, D3). The eight members of the tribunal, in their black peasant smocks, each represent one of the main irrigation channels that bring water to the rich *huerta* (the fertile agricultural plain). They're here to settle local farmers' irrigation disputes. Proceedings are in Valenciano and exclusively oral – no written record is kept – and fines are expressed in *lliures valencianes,* a long defunct local currency. In reality, there are rarely any complaints and its all rather anticlimactic. ⊠ Plaza de la Virgen ⏲ noon, Thu only ⊜ 8, 9, 16, 28, 71

VALENCIA FOR CHILDREN

Children's Mini Road Layout (2, F2)

Within the Jardines del Real, there's a miniature road system, complete with traffic signs and bridges. You have to take your own bike, trike or pedal car, but it's great fun – and a learning experience too. ⊠ Calle General Élio € free ⏲ 6.30am-9pm Apr-Sep, 8.30am-8.30pm Oct-Mar ⊜ 1, 26, 32, 79, 81 ♿ good

Gulliver (3, D3)

Lilliputian kids scramble, clamber and slide all over a magnificent, ever-patient Gulliver (gooly-*vare*) reclining in the river bed. In the unlikely event that yours

BABY-SITTING

Most top-end hotels and quite a few other hotels can find a baby-sitter for you if you give them advance notice.

The Tribunal de las Aguas (opposite) has been solving Water Court disputes for 1000 years...

get bored, nearby there's minigolf, a conventional playground, a skateboard ramp and a giant chessboard.
☎ 96 337 02 04 ✉ Paseo de la Alameda s/n € free ☺ 10am-8pm Sep-Jun, 10am-2pm & 5-9pm Jul & Aug 🚌 18, 19, 40, 95 ♿ fair

Jardín Zoológico (2, E1)
Highlights of Valencia's small zoo, within the Jardines del Real, include the animals of the night pavilion and a drop-dead-gorgeous orang-utan called Boris. Once the vast Bioparc de Valencia is ready to welcome them in 2007, the animals will move upriver to their new, hugely improved, more spacious home.
☎ 96 360 08 22 ✉ Calle San Pío V s/n € €5/2.50 ☺ 10am-sunset 🚌 1, 26, 32, 79, 81 ♿ fair

Teatro de Marionetas La Estrella (3, A1)
Within the large Espai Campanar shopping centre, La Estrella Puppet Theatre has been delighting children for over a decade. Its other **theatre** (4, A2; ☎ 96 356 22 92; Calle Los Ángeles 33) has shows at 6.30pm, Saturday and Sunday.
☎ 96 356 22 92 🖳 www .teatrolaestrella.com in Spanish ✉ Centro Comercial Espai Campanar, Avenida Tirso de Molina 16 € €7/5 ☺ performances at 5pm & 6.30pm Sat & Sun 🚌 17, 95

TO SHARE WITH MUM & DAD
Other things to see and do that are especially good for families:
- A carriage ride (p29)
- Flying a kite (p29)
- Free Sunday morning theatre for children at the Museo Prehistórico y de las Culturas de Valencia (p23)
- Golondrinas Transvimar (p29)
- Jardín Botánico (p28; watch out for the feral cats!)
- Jardines del Turia, especially the Parque de la Cabecera (p28)
- Las Arenas and La Malvarrosa beaches (p16)
- Museo de Historia de Valencia (p15)
- Museo del Artista Fallero (p22)
- The high-speed tram (p82)
- Oceanogràfic (p10)

Trips & Tours

WALKING TOURS
Around Centro Histórico

This whistle-stop walk takes you past the historic quarter's major monuments. It could easily take a whole day if you explore each one.

From **Plaza de la Virgen** (**1**; p8), briefly head west along Calle Caballeros, main thoroughfare of medieval Valencia. Turn right into Calle Serranos; the peeling *Refugio* sign above **No 25** (**2**) indicates an old Spanish Civil War air-raid shelter. At Plaza de los Fueros and the massive **Torres de Serranos** (**3**; p17), go left into Calle Roteros to **Plaza del Carmen** (**4**; p27), where the façade of the old **Iglesia del Carmen** (**5**; p25) and **Palacio de Pineda** (**6**) stare each other out. Turn left (south) into Calle Pintor Fillol, which becomes Calle Baja (Low Street). This and its twin, Calle Alta (you've guessed it, 'High Street') were also important medieval thoroughfares.

At **Plaza del Tossal** (**7**; p27), pause for a drink in **San Jaume** (**8**; p62) then continue down Calle Bolsería. Turn left into Plaza del Mercado to visit **La Lonja** (**9**; p13) and **Mercado Central** (**10**; p14).

Bear right at the junction with Calle San Vicente Mártir, detouring briefly to look at the **Town Hall** (**11**; p27) and **Central Post Office** (**12**; p24) in **Plaza del Ayuntamiento** (**13**; p27). Returning, head north up Calle San Vicente Mártir to **Plaza de la Reina** (**14**), soulless but for a few cafés. Slip up the lane that runs to the left (west) of the cathedral to get back to your starting point.

Distance 3km **Duration** 1hr
▶ **Start** Ⓜ Plaza de la Virgen
● **End** Ⓜ Plaza de la Virgen

Take time to admire the Modernista interior of Mercado Central

Modernismo Meander

This walk takes in Valencia's main Modernista (a primarily Catalan movement, similar to Art Nouveau) buildings. After sniffing around the **Mercado Central** (**1**; p14), take in the elaborate stucco façade of **Calle Ramilletes 1** (**2**). Follow Avenida María Cristina to Plaza del Ayuntamiento and the **Central Post Office** (**3**; p24). At the end of Calle Ribera, detour briefly to the **Estación del Norte** (**4**; p19). Take Calle Russafa, then turn left for **Casa Ortega** (**5**; Gran Vía Marqués del Turia 9) with its elaborate floral decoration. Go left along Calle Félix Pizcueta, then first right, stopping at **Casa Ferrer** (**6**; Calle Cirilo Amorós 29), garlanded with swags of stucco roses and ceramic tiling. Continue northwards to **Mercado de Colón** (**7**, p25), a good spot for a drink, then head west to the **Casa del Dragón** (**8**; Calle Jorge Juan 3), named for its dragon motifs.

Cross Calle Colón, turn right along Calle Poeta Quintana, pass the impressive mounted statue of King Jaime I and join Calle Paz. In the 19th century **Nos 42–44** (**9**) were the Palace Hotel, Valencia's finest. Under restoration, they'll again function as a hotel. **No 31** (**10**) has an elaborate *mirador* (corner balcony), and intertwined stucco wreaths and olive branches. **No 36** (**11**), nowadays the Nest youth hostel, has even more delicate leafy iron railings.

At the end of Calle Paz, continue straight, maybe calling in for an *horchata* (Valencian drink made from tiger nuts) at **Horchatería Santa Catalina** (**12**; p49). Then, at Plaza Lope de Vega, turn left into Calle Trench to return to the Mercado Central.

Distance 3.5km **Duration** 45min
▶ **Start** Mercado Central
● **End** Mercado Central

Central Post Office, Plaza del Ayuntamiento

Green Valencia

Within this busy city, you can hop from park to park, and garden to garden, following the Jardines del Turia along the old river bed.

Begin by savouring the intimate formal charm of **Jardín de Monforte** (**1**; p28). Exiting, go right, then left up the broad central, planted reservation of Avenida Blasco Ibáñez and enter the **Jardines del Real** (**2**; p28). After 75m, turn left beside two large **cages** (**3**) of parrots, budgerigars and native birds. If you're with children, you might want to detour to the **Jardín Zoológico** (**4**; p31) or **Museo de Ciencias Naturales** (**5**; p22), both within the park.

Continuing, exit by the park's main southern gate and go through the short foot tunnel to the **Jardines del Turia** (**6**; p28). Turn right, upstream, passing the **Torres de Serranos** (**7**; p17), a baseball diamond and **rugby pitch** (**8**), following the

Time for a quick review of *Best of Valencia*!

river bed under five bridges. Enjoy a restorative drink at the small **café** (**9**) below the bus station. Cross to the south bank and climb the stone ramp (once used to roll logs for the sawmills of the Barrio del Carmen).

In front of you is the **Jardín de los Hespérides** (**10**; p28) but you'll have to double back 150m to cross busy Paseo de la Pechina at the traffic lights. After visiting the gardens, go down cobbled Calle Gaspar Bono. At the end of the long wall on your left, turn left at Calle Quart for the entrance to **Jardín Botánico** (**11**; p28).

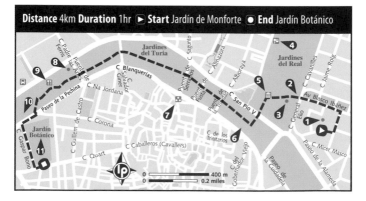

Distance 4km **Duration** 1hr ▶ **Start** Jardín de Monforte ● **End** Jardín Botánico

DAY TRIPS
La Albufera (1, B3)

For a fun day out, visit La Albufera, a wide freshwater lagoon about 15km south of Valencia, building in a paella lunch and boat trip at the village of El Palmar. Some 90 bird species regularly nest around its shores while more than 250 use it as a migratory staging post. Separated from the sea by a narrow strip of sand dunes and pine forest, its waters are scarcely 1m deep; hence the distinctive flat-bottomed boats used to harvest fish and eels. Look too for *barracas* – typical Albufera houses that have steeply pitched, thatched roofs.

INFORMATION
15km south of Valencia

🚌 Valencia Bus Turístico; Autocares Herca (€1.60, one hour)

ⓘ Racó de l'Olla Visitors Centre (☎ 96 162 73 45; Carretera el Palmar s/n)

✕ L'Establiment (☎ 96 162 01 00; Camino Estell, El Palmar)

The **Racó de l'Olla visitors centre** (admission free; ☙ 9am-2pm, 4-5.30pm Tue & Thu Oct-Jun, 4-6.30pm Tue & Thu Jul-Sep) has an informative pamphlet in English, a guided walk, a bird-watching hide and visitor-operated closed-circuit TV cameras.

El Palmar seems almost all restaurants and, indeed, catering has overtaken fishing as its main source of income. More than 30 in a village of fewer than 1200 inhabitants serve paella and *all i pebre* – eels, hauled wriggling from the lake and simmered in a garlic rich peppery stew.

A boat trip on the lake costs around €4 per person with a minimum of €12 per boat.

Five to seven daily Autocares Herca buses serve El Palmar via El Saler. Valencia Bus Turístico (p37) is a more convenient option. At other than peak times, you can hop off in El Palmar, then catch a later bus back to Valencia.

Explore the wonders of paella in El Palmar

Sagunto (1, B1)

Sagunto was a thriving Iberian community (called – infelicitously, with hindsight – Arse) as early as the 5th century BC, minting its own coins and trading with both Greeks and Phoenicians. In 219 BC Hannibal, on the epic journey that lead him and his elephants over the Alps towards Rome, besieged the town. Rather than capitulating, the inhabitants chose mass suicide and their town was razed, sparking the Second Punic War between Carthage and Rome. Rome won, named the town Saguntum and set about rebuilding it.

INFORMATION
25km north of Valencia

🚉 Sagunto; €1.65, 30 minutes

ℹ tourist office (☎ 96 266 22 13; Plaza del Cronista Chabret)

✖ Armeler (☎ 96 266 43 82; Calle Subida al Castillo 44)

From the train station it's a 10-minute walk to the tourist office. A further 15-minute uphill walk – detour briefly into **Judería**, the former Jewish quarter – brings you to the over-restored 1st-century **Roman theatre**.

Higher up, the **fortress complex** (admission free; ⏲ 10am-dusk Tue-Sat, 10am-2pm Sun), mostly in ruins, was constructed, modified and added to over centuries. Winding around the hillside for almost a kilometre, its highlights include the well-preserved Plaza de Armas, left (east) of the main entrance, and, beyond it, the massive Muslim gateway of the Plaza de Almenara. There's also a small Antiquarium Epigráfico, a collection of mainly Roman inscriptions. But the real charm of a ramble through the tangle of cactuses and chaos of shaped stones is the spectacular panorama of the town, coast and green sea of orange groves.

Behind this fortress is a wonderful panorama – why not see for yourself?

ORGANISED TOURS

When it comes to tours of the organised kind, Valencia is very much a do-it-yourself city. You'll find it more profitable to concoct your own programme, except for the following options. If your Spanish is up to it, you'll also glean more from a horse-drawn carriage ride (p29) or a harbour boat trip with Golondrinas Transvimar (p29). Orange Bikes (p82) also offers bike tours of the city in English, Spanish and German.

Valencia Bus Turístico (2, D4)

Fluorescent orange, difficult to-miss buses do a 90 minute circuit of the city's most important sights with recorded English commentary. Tickets are valid for 24

hours and you can hop off and on at four significant sites: Instituto Valenciano de Arte Moderno (IVAM), Ciudad de las Artes y las Ciencias, Oceanogràfic and Museo de Bellas Artes. It also does a similar two-hour tour of La Albufera (p35), including a half-hour boat trip on the lake. Check with the driver; except at times of peak demand, you can linger in El Palmar and take a later bus back.

☎ 96 341 44 00 💻 www .valenciabusturistic.com in Spanish ✉ Plaza de la Reina € €12/6 🕒 approximately half-hourly 10.30am-9pm Apr-Oct, hourly 10.30am-7.30pm Nov-Mar

Valencia Guías (3, B2)

Each Saturday at 10am, Valencia Guías leads 3½-hour cycle tours of town (in both Spanish and English), leaving from its premises. Reserve in advance. There are also

two-hour walking tours of the historic heart of town. Guided in Spanish and English, they depart from the main entrance of the Town Hall in Plaza del Ayuntamiento (2, C5). Reserve at major travel agencies or just turn up.

☎ 96 385 17 40 💻 www .valenciaguias.com ✉ Paseo de la Pechina 32 € €22 🕒 at 10am Sat

Shopping

Famed Francis Montesinos' boutique (p40)

It's well worth leaving plenty of space in your luggage for a spot of indulgent clothes shopping. You'll find the prices at Spanish international chains such as Zara, Mango and Massimo Dutti are up to a third less than, for example, in the UK. Footwear too can be a real bargain and the city has enough shops to shoe an army. What's just as much fun is poking around the small, independent clothing boutiques for something you can be certain your best friend won't be wearing. See p40 for a list of some of the Barrio del Carmen's best, all conveniently concentrated in a tight triangle of streets and easily browsed in an hour or so.

Less easy to find are small shops, alas these days extinct in many European countries, that specialise in a single product (we know of one dusty place that manages to survive solely on balls of string and hanks of rope). You'll find some of our favourite shops with character on pp41–3.

On the food front, look out for signs indicating *mantequerías* and *ultramarinos*, fast-disappearing, individually owned delicatessens and purveyors of exotic foods (*ultramarinos* means 'from across the seas'). Jars and cans are stacked from floor to ceiling and they're often the best places to buy cheese and wines.

WHERE TO SHOP

Nearly every building on Calle Colón (2, D6 & E5) is a shop. Along its length you'll find everything from a trio of branches of Corte Inglés, the nationwide chain store, to trendy boutiques. For really fashionable clothes and gorgeous displays that make window shopping a pleasure in itself, browse Calle Conde Salvatierra, Calle Jorge Juan and intersecting Calle Sorní. Elsewhere, Calle Poeta Querol has a branch of Spanish top-end designer Loewe and international labels with tip-top prices such as Louis Vuitton, Hermès and Ermenegildo Zegna.

CLOTHING & SHOE SIZES

Women's Clothing

Aust/UK	8	10	12	14	16	18
Europe	36	38	40	42	44	46
Japan	5	7	9	11	13	15
USA	6	8	10	12	14	16

Women's Shoes

Aust/USA	5	6	7	8	9	10
Europe	35	36	37	38	39	40
France only	35	36	38	39	40	42
Japan	22	23	24	25	26	27
UK	3½	4½	5½	6½	7½	8½

Men's Clothing

Aust	92	96	100	104	108	112
Europe	46	48	50	52	54	56

Japan	S	M	M		L	
UK/USA	35	36	37	38	39	40

Men's Shirts (Collar Sizes)

Aust/Japan	38	39	40	41	42	43
Europe	38	39	40	41	42	43
UK/USA	15	15½	16	16½	17	17½

Men's Shoes

Aust/UK	7	8	9	10	11	12
Europe	41	42	43	44½	46	47
Japan	26	27	27.5	28	29	30
USA	7½	8½	9½	10½	11½	12½

Measurements approximate only; try before you buy.

CLOTHING & SHOES

Valencia's annual Pasarela del Carmen fashion collection can't yet rival the catwalks of say Barcelona or Madrid. Even so, there's some pretty slinky stuff to be searched out, whether in the shops of the most prominent Spanish designers, around the chic city boutiques or within the trendiest of the national chains (see p40).

Alex Vidal (2, E6)
Local designer Alex Vidal has his smart new two-storey shop and headquarters here. He sells women's haute couture, shoes and accessories that bear his own label, and also some Italian-brand items that he's designed. There are branches of Alex Vidal at Calle Sorní 6 (2, E5) and Calle de Salvá 2 (2, D5).
☎ 96 342 73 37 🖳 www .alexvidal.es ✉ Calle Hernán Cortés 13 ◷ 10am-1.30pm & 4.30-8pm Mon-Fri, 10.30am-2pm & 5-8.30pm Sat 🚍 5, 10, 13, 32, 81

Alfredo Esteve (2, E6)
Twice a year, Alfredo Esteve travels to Italy to select his offerings for the following season. His are the only shops in Valencia where you'll find designer labels such as Gucci, Prada and Dolce & Gabbana for men: classic lines at No 18, sport and leisure wear at No 32.
☎ 96 374 08 38, 96 374 08 38 ✉ Gran Vía Marqués de Turia 18 & 32 ◷ 10am-2pm & 5-8.30pm Mon-Sat 🚍 1, 2, 63, 79, 80

Beguer (2, E5)
Local enterprise Beguer manufactures in Torrente, a dormitory town southwest of Valencia. It sells mainly its own fashionable shoes and boots for men and women, plus a range of other labels. There's also a branch at Calle Hernán Cortés 16 (2, E6).
☎ 96 394 25 47 🖳 www .beguer.com ✉ Calle Colón 58 ◷ 10am-8.45pm Mon-Sat 🚍 5, 10, 13, 32, 81

INSIDER TRADING

Psst, here's a tip. Find the first building on the left (No 1) of Pasaje Doctor Serra, a covered gallery running alongside the bullring. Go up the stairs, turn right and there, in an unassuming office (No 3), you'll find **Alex Vidal Stocks** (2, D6; ☎ 96 352 87 55; ◷ 10am-1.30pm & 4.30-8pm Mon-Fri, 10.30am-2pm Sat), where discounts on previous year's stock *begin* at 60%.

Camper (2, D6)
Mallorca-based shoe company Camper is something of a Spanish institution. But just because it's popular doesn't mean that its output is run-of-the-mill. Choose what fits you and you'll dance out, toes tapping with satisfaction.
☎ 96 353 39 55 🖳 www
.camper.com ✉ Calle Colón 13 🕑 10am-9pm Mon-Sat 🚍 5, 10, 13, 32, 81

Francis Montesinos
(2, F5)
The doyen of Valencian fashion designers, the eponymous, internationally acclaimed Francis Montesinos has only one retail outlet. The shop, selling mainly women's haute couture plus a few items for men, is a work of art in itself.
☎ 96 394 06 12 🖳 www
.francismontesinos.com in Spanish ✉ Calle Conde Salvatierra 25 🕑 10am-2pm & 5-8.30pm Mon-Sat 🚍 4, 5, 10, 12, 13

Mi Talón de Aquiles (2, A6)
This smart boutique retails trendy women's attire bearing national labels such as Boba from Madrid, Catalan Josep Sant and Valencia's own Alexandro Sáez de la Torre. You'll also find European brands Jacamola, Trussardi and Petit Bateau.
☎ 96 327 09 64 🖳 www
.mitalondeaquiles.com in Spanish ✉ Calle Cuenca 38B 🕑 10.30am-2pm & 5-8.30pm Mon-Sat 🚍 1, 2, 41, 79, 80

Porfin (2, A3)
Hip Valencian designer Alexandro Sáez de la Torre's

CHIC BOUTIQUES

Until about five years ago, there was scarcely a small clothes shop anyone younger than your mum would be seen dead in. Nowadays, fresh, sassy boutiques sprout and flower almost by the month. Here's just a selection of favourites, easily visited in a short triangular stroll within the Barrio del Carmen. Opening hours tend to be from 9am or 10am to 2pm, then from 5pm to 8pm.

Bacilacoco (2, C3; ☎ 96 392 07 69; Calle Purisima 5) 'Only fashion victims', they proclaim at this hip spot for women's fashions and accessories. Might you qualify?

Cactus (2, C4; ☎ 661 407467; Calle Derechos 35) Maureen O'Callaghan (as Spanish as they come despite her Celtic name) scours Asia, Europe and her homeland for fetching women's fashions and accessories.

Hakuna Matata (2, C3; ☎ 617 952635; Calle Calatrava 4) A fair trader, it makes its own jewellery and other artefacts, and buys in directly from fellow artists.

Mil Ranas (2, C3; ☎ 96 391 43 16; Calle Correjeria 20) Sole rep in Valencia of the Basque fashion house Skunk Funk. Cool clothing for him.

Mil Ranas (2, C4; ☎ 96 391 11 07; Plaza Virgen de la Paz 2) Equivalent of the above for her.

Monki (2, C3; ☎ 96 392 45 16; www.monkishop.com in Spanish; Calle Calatrava 11) Lisa, the Irish owner, has a keen eye for fads and fashions, buying in from local designers and combing Europe for striking women's wear.

Sine Die (2, C3; ☎ 96 315 20 35; www.sine-die.com in Spanish; Calle Correjeria 4) More upmarket, all its items are confected in Spain and conceived by young Spanish designers.

---

label is Porfin. Here, he has his studio, where he designs and displays his creations for both men and women.
☎ 96 373 53 22
🖳 porfin2@inicia.es
✉ Door 4, Calle Guillem de Castro 96 🕑 10am-2pm & 4.30-8.30pm Mon-Fri 🚍 5

STYLISH SPANISH CHAINS

Adolfo Dominguez (2, E5)
Originating in Galicia, and now international and specialising in both men's

and women's clothes, shoes and accessories, Adolfo Dominguez offers exquisite materials, quality tailoring and garments that will stand the test of time. There's another branch at Calle Sorní 3 (2, F5).
☎ 96 394 48 31 🖳 www
.adolfodominguez.es
✉ Calle Colón 52
🕑 10.30am-9pm Mon-Sat 🚍 4, 5, 10, 12, 13

Bañon (2, E5)
Another all-Valencian outfit Bañon selects its wares from

all over the world. It sells women's clothing, chic household ware, mock furs, kids' cuddly toys, doormats, watering cans and whatever else takes its fancy. There's a branch nearby at Calle Jorge Juan 5, plus three others around town. ☎ 96 352 82 46 🖳 www .banon.es ✉ Calle Jorge Juan 13 ⏲ 11.30am-2pm & 4.30-8.30pm Mon-Sat 🚌 5, 10, 13, 32, 81

Mango (2, E5)

Like Zara, Mango is a Spanish company that these days has branches worldwide. It's a bit funkier than its rival, blending sassy couture with quality fabrics and department-store prices. There are branches in shopping centres and at Calle Juan de Austria 7 (2, D5). ☎ 96 352 88 58 🖳 www .mango.es ✉ Calle Colón 31 ⏲ 10am-9pm Mon-Sat 🚌 4, 5, 10, 12, 13

ALPARGATAS

A pair of *alpargatas* (traditional *valenciano* farmer's footwear – canvas on top with a sole of dried, woven grasses and bound to the ankle by cross-gartered tape) makes an original present for the folks back home and a practical alternative to sandals, especially where it's sandy or dusty.

Massimo Dutti (2, D6)

Despite the Italian name Massimo Dutti is as Spanish as flamenco (it's part of the Zara conglomerate). There are twin shops: look left for men's clothing and right for women's wear. It has branches in all the big shopping centres and at Calle Juan de Austria 4 (2, D5). ☎ 96 352 42 63 🖳 www .massimodutti.com ✉ Calle Colón 9 ⏲ 10am-9pm Mon-Sat 🚌 4, 5, 10, 12, 13

Zara (2, D6)

With several branches around town, Zara sells smart, quality, inexpensive casuals. These two branches are bang opposite each other; both have men's and women's departments while No 11 does great gear for fashion-conscious kids. ☎ 96 352 76 03, 96 352 68 13 🖳 www.zara.com ✉ Calle Colón 11 & 18 ⏲ 10am-9pm Mon-Sat 🚌 5, 10, 13, 32, 81

Zara Home (2, F5)

The household items in Zara Home have the same flair for design and reasonable prices as the original Zara fashion chain. You'll find very modish sheets, blankets, cutlery, crockery, baskets and suchlike – and there's great recorded jazz blowing in the background. ☎ 96 351 32 52 🖳 www .zarahome.com ✉ Calle Jorge Juan 15 ⏲ 10am-9pm Mon-Sat 🚌 5, 10, 13, 32, 81

LOCAL SPECIALISTS & ODDITIES

One of the pleasant things about Spain, in general, and Valencia, in particular, is that the small, specialist, single-product shops still manage to cling on despite heavyweight competition from all-purpose department stores.

Abanicos Carbonell
(3, C3)

For handmade fans with true cachet, visit this splendid little place, where the same family has been producing them in the rear workshop for five generations. Pick up a trim hand-painted item for around €20, buy one for as little as €1 (yes, truly) or invest over €300.

☎ 96 341 53 95 ▯ www .abanicoscarbonell.com ✉ Calle Castellón 21 ◔ 9.30am-1.30pm & 4-8pm Mon-Fri ▭ 1, 2, 3, 7, 8, 9, 40, 79, 80

Delve into Cestería Alemany, where more is better

Casa de los Dulces (2, D2)

For more than 50 years, the Sweet House has been selling technicolour lollipops, sweets and candies that stretch and pull, loose, wrapped or boxed. There are also more than 100 jars, each holding a different variety of boiled sweet and enough to satisfy the most demanding child.

☎ 96 391 93 41 ✉ Calle Muro de Santa Ana 6 ◔ 9.30am-2pm & 4.30-9pm Mon-Sat, 9am-3pm & 5-9pm Sun ▭ 2, 5, 28, 80, 95

Casa de los Falleros (2, B5)

Here's the place to buy a traditional *fallera* (female participant in Las Fallas) dress and accessories, or simply see roll upon roll of embroidered, sequined cloth and racks of off-the peg dresses. Flex your credit card; a ready-made ensemble will set you back at least €700 while a special creation could climb to €4000.

☎ 96 352 14 00 ✉ Calle Quevedo 6 ◔ 9.30am-1.30pm & 4.30-8pm Mon-Fri, 10am-2pm & 5-8pm Sat ▭ 5, 60, 62, 70

Cestería Alemany (2, C4)

This wonderfully cluttered shop sells everything woven from whippy wood and straw: baskets, boxes, trunks, screens, racks and more. The lightweight esparto-grass slippers (€6) make original presents, easily tucked into your luggage. Along the same street, **El Globo** (2, C4; Musico Peydro 16), more cramped, piles its wicker goods just as high.

☎ 96 352 11 92 ✉ Calle Liñan 8 ◔ 10am-2pm & 5-8pm Mon-Sat ▭ 7, 27, 28, 81

COOL FANS, WARM SHAWLS

Two other places, both very central, to pick up a special fan – are **Nela** (2, D4; Calle San Vicente Mártir 2), which also does a nice line in umbrellas and walking sticks, and **Rosalén** (2, D4; Calle San Vicente Mártir 19). Both stock gorgeous Manila shawls, which vary in price from around €40 for a simple, machine-spun version to as much as €300 for a special silk number.

Cuchilleria Eureka (2, D4)
Eureka indeed! If you've left your shaving kit at home, Cuchilleria Eureka carries around 400 varieties of shaving brush, more toe-clippers than you have toes, plus nose tweezers and other essential accoutrements for the person about town. The window display might be a surgeon's outfitters.
☎ 96 352 06 01 ✉ Calle San Vicente Mártir 3 ✪ 10am-2pm & 5-8pm Mon-Sat 🚌 4, 8, 9, 31, 70

Guantes Camps (2, D4)
In a city where the temperature rarely tumbles below 0°C, this little shop specialises in gloves for all occasions: from cycling and skiing to weddings and horse riding. They'll gently rest your elbow on a soft cushion and ease one on for size. There's a similar shop (same name, different owners) at Calle San Vicente Mártir 3.
☎ 96 392 39 81 ✉ Plaza de la Reina 18 ✪ 9am-1.15pm & 5-8pm Mon-Sat 🚌 4, 8, 9, 31, 70

Sombreros Albero

EL RASTRILLO
Each Sunday between 10am and 4pm, Valencia's largest flea market spreads over Plaza Luis Casanova (3, D2), in the shadow of the stands of Valencia Club de Fútbul's stadium. Much of the stuff looks as though it's been hauled out of someone's rubbish bin but, among the gypsy scrap and secondhand tat, you might root out an antique bargain, and there are certainly plenty of quirky potential presents for folk back home.

Sombreros Albero (2, D6)
Sombreros Albero can set you up with a dapper panama, trilby, beret or bonnet? Most of what's on sale has been knocked up locally by this small concern, in the hands of the Albero family since 1820. There's also a **branch** (2, C4; Plaza del Mercado 9) beside the central market.
☎ 96 351 22 45 ✉ Calle Xàtiva 21 ✪ 10am-1.30pm & 5-8pm Mon-Sat Ⓜ Xàtiva 🚌 5, 10, 13, 32, 81

FOOD & DRINK

Bodega Beal's (2, A6)
Cross to the Gran Vía's less fashionable side to explore this wonderful specialist shop. As a delicatessen, it's unimpressive. But it carries a huge range of spirits and aisle upon aisle of wines, nudging 2000 different bottles, from palatable and costing less than €3.50 to sky's-the-limit finest vintages.
☎ 96 385 52 49 ✉ Calle Alcira 15 ✪ 9am-1.45pm & 5-8.30pm Mon-Sat 🚌 1, 2, 3, 79, 80

Bombonerías Nuatté (2, C3)
This little shop specialises in rich chocolates. For an original take-home present, if you can keep your fingers off them, buy a box of the round chocs embossed – in chocolate – with the city's major monuments. There's another branch in the Mercado de Colón (p25).
☎ 96 391 37 91 ✉ Calle Caballeros 4 ✪ 10am-2pm & 5-8.30pm Mon Sat, 11.30am 2pm Sun 🚌 4, 6, 16, 28, 70

Caçao Sampaka (2, F5)
Here's a temple to cocoa and all that can be fashioned from it. Indulge yourself with a packet of handmade chocolates, all made from pure, unadulterated cocoa, such as the Collección Gaudí, chocolates in the soft shapes and spun whorls that were the trademark of the famous Catalan architect.
☎ 96 353 40 62 🖥 www .cacaosampaka.com in Spanish ✉ Calle Conde Salvatierra 19 ✪ 9am-9pm Mon-Fri, 10am-9pm Sat 🚌 4, 5, 10, 12, 13

Las Añadas de España (2, C6)
The Seasons of Spain is a true temple to gourmet food. It carries the very best in cheeses, cold meats, pâtés and sausages and does delicious cakes and desserts. It

TURRÓN

This particularly lip-smacking variant upon nougat makes a great, local, handy-sized present to take home. Traditionally eaten only around Christmas time, it's a treat at any time of the year. There are two main kinds: *turrón de Jijona*, soft and fudge like; and *turrón de Alicante*, altogether crispier and crunchier. **Turrones Ramos** (☎ 96 392 33 98; Sombería 11) sells *turrón* from its own factory in Jijona.

has an ample wine selection, and also offers Saturday wine-tasting courses for €35 per person.
☎ 96 353 38 45 🖳 www .lasanadas.es in Spanish ✉ Calle Xàtiva 3 🕑 10am-2pm & 5-8.30pm Mon-Sat 🚌 5, 27, 71

Mantequerías Vicente Castillo (3, C3)
Mantequerías (old-style grocer shops and delicatessens) are gradually giving up in the face of supermarket competition. But not Vicente Castillo's. Established in 1916, it boasts Valencia's largest wine cellar with over 12,000 bottles and offers the finest

cheeses, sausages and shelves of cans and jars crammed with gastro-exotica.
☎ 96 351 04 23 ✉ Gran Vía Marques del Turia 1 🕑 9am-2pm & 5-8.30pm Mon-Sat 🚌 1, 8, 40, 79, 80

Martinez (2, D6)
Just smell the aroma of sweet chocolate wafting through from the rear oven! Over 75 years, Martinez has perfected its melt-in-the-mouth truffles, marrons glacés and rich, dark, handmade chocolates. The packaging is almost as elegant as the treasures within.
☎ 96 351 62 89 🖳 www .trufasmartinez.com in

Spanish ✉ Calle Russafa 12 🕑 9am-2pm & 4-8pm Mon-Fri, 9.30am-2.30pm Sat 🚌 5, 10, 13, 32, 81

Navarro (2, C5)
A little west of Plaza del Ayuntamiento, Navarro is Valencia's best option for vegetarian food, including organic vegetables. It carries a wide range of products from around Europe and, if you're in town for long enough, will take orders for items not in stock.
☎ 96 352 28 51 ✉ Calle Arzobispo Mayoral 20 🕑 9am-2pm & 5-8pm Mon-Sat Ⓜ Xàtiva

Villanueva (2, D5)
Run by the same family since 1947, Villanueva is widely renowned for its cakes and pastries. Everything you see has been created in the bakery behind the shop. It's also a popular drop-in place if you want to pick up a mid-morning cake or *bocadillo* (French-bread sandwich).

Las Añadas de España (p43) is regarded by many shoppers as a temple for tummies

And then there's choccies...

☎ 96 351 03 41 ✉ Calle Juan de Austria 28 🕓 9.30am-3pm & 5-9pm Mon-Sat, 9.30am-3pm Sun 🚌 5, 6, 10, 13, 81

BOOKS & MUSIC

Discos Amsterdam (3, B1)
Juan Vitoria, author, journalist and broadcaster, started this magnificent music shop 25 years ago. Plastered with posters, it specialises in indie titles and the seriously retro and rare. It will undertake searches and accepts Internet orders. It's opposite the fashion shop Zara, on the lower level of the Nuevo Centro shopping centre.
☎ 96 348 39 65 🖳 www .arrakis.es/~jvitoria/Amst erdam in Spanish ✉ Local 80, Lower Level, Centro Comercial el Nuevo Centro, Avenida Pío XII 2 🕓 10am-7pm Mon-Sat 🚇 Turia

Casa del Llibre (2, D6)
Offspring of the giant Madrid mother store, the Home of the Book is the best general bookshop in town. In the basement there's a reasonable stock of titles in English, French and other major languages, and a good selection of guidebooks, mostly in Spanish.
☎ 96 353 00 80 🖳 www .casadellibro.com in Spanish ✉ Passeig Russafa 11 🕓 10am-9.30pm Mon-Sat, noon-9.30pm Sun 🚇 Xàtiva 🚌 5, 10, 13, 32, 81

Fnac (2, B6)
This huge chain department store, French in origin, has Valencia's largest selection of CDs. It carries a decent range of books and has smallish English literature and guidebook sections, the latter with some Lonely Planet titles.
☎ 96 353 90 00 🖳 www .fnac.es in Spanish ✉ Calle Guillem de Castro 9-11 🕓 10am-9.30pm Mon-Sat, noon-9.30pm Sun 🚇 Xàtiva 🚌 5, 27, 71

IVAM Bookshop (2, A2)
If you're looking for a coffee-table art book or some stylish bauble to take home, the Instituto Valenciano de Arte Moderno contemporary art gallery (IVAM; p12) has a great shop.
☎ 96 386 30 00 ✉ Calle Guillem de Castro 118 🕓 10am-8pm Tue-Sun Oct-May, 10am-10pm Tue-Sun Jun-Sep 🚌 5, 28, 80, 95

Librería Patagonia (2, D2)
Patagonia is an excellent little travel bookshop with an unrivalled selection of maps, guidebooks, climbing and trekking manuals, mostly in Spanish. Exceptionally friendly and helpful, it also carries some guidebooks in English, including lots of Lonely Planet titles.
☎ 96 393 60 52 🖳 www .libreriapatagonia.com in Spanish ✉ Calle Santa Amalia 2 🕓 10am-1.30pm & 4.30-8.30pm Mon-Fri, 10am-2pm Sat 🚇 Pont de Fusta

READING ABOUT VALENCIA

To get a feel for the Valencia of not so many yesterdays ago, pick up one of the novels of Blasco Ibañez, many of them translated into English. His most famous title outside Spain is *The Four Horsemen of the Apocalypse*, first filmed starring Rudolph Valentino. He writes with deep insight about both bourgeois urban life and that of the peasants and fisherfolk of La Albufera (see p35).

For something with much more of a today feel, three books that treat contemporary Spain with great sensitivity – and, more than incidentally, Valencia too, where he lives – are Jason Webster's bestselling *Duende*, *Andalus* and his latest, *Guerra: Living in the Shadows of the Spanish Civil War*.

Eating

Valencia is the capital of *la huerta*, a fertile coastal agricultural plain that supplies the city with delightfully fresh fruit and vegetables. It's a fishing port as well, so the bounty of the sea also comes direct and fresh to your table.

Rice is the staple of much Valencian cuisine – and the basis of paella, the dish that Valencia exported to the world. Other local favourites include *arroz a banda* (rice simmered in a fish stock), *arroz negro* (rice with squid, simmered in its ink) and *arroz al horno* (rice baked in the oven). And then there's *fideuá*, a tasty paella made with noodles instead of rice.

LA CUENTA, POR FAVOR (THE BILL/CHECK, PLEASE)

The price symbols used in this chapter are based upon a full meal (starter, main and dessert) for one person, excluding drinks.

€€€€	over €40
€€€	€31–40
€€	€16–30
€	up to €15

Contrary to the national stereotype, *valencianos* aren't big on tapas. Yes, they'll very often ask for a tapa to accompany a drink and soak up the alcohol but, there's little tradition of floating from bar to bar, picking here and picking there. But most bars offer plenty of snacky bites and we've recommended several places that are particularly renowned for their tapas – and where you can also go for a full meal.

Rice is a national staple and the basis of a good paella

BARRIO DEL CARMEN

Ana Eva (2, A3)
Vegetarian €€
The smartest of Valencia's limited vegetarian options has a tasteful décor and delightful rear patio, open in summer and covered in cooler months. They prepare some very imaginative dishes and do great juices. With starters including rice, pasta, potatoes and couscous, you won't walk out rumbling.
☎ 96 391 53 69 ✉ Calle Turia 49 🕙 lunch Tue-Sun, dinner Tue-Sat 🚌 5, 7, 81, 95 ♿ good **V**

Bar Pilar (2, B3)
Tapas €
Bar Pilar is famed for its mussels. Ask for an *entero* – a platterful in a spicy broth that you scoop up with a spare shell. At the bar, etiquette demands that you dump your empty shells in the plastic trough at your feet. Although cramped, it's also excellent for tapas.
☎ 96 391 04 97 ✉ Calle Moro Zeit 13 🕙 noon-midnight 🚌 5B ♿ fair

Ca'an Bermell (2, B2)
Tapas €€
Baleful-eyed fish and tumbling seafood packed in ice fill Ca'an Bermell's window. This traditional restaurant,

Roll out the barrels at Ca'an Bermell – it has great seafood

with its simple wooden tables and benches, has been serving the freshest of tapas to discerning *valencianos* for over 25 years. In season, it offers all kinds of wild mushrooms and dishes seasoned with wild truffles.
☎ 96 391 02 88 ✉ Calle Santo Tomás 18 🕙 lunch Tue-Sat, dinner Mon-Sat 🚌 5, 5B, 27, 80, 95 ♿ fair

Chust Godoy (2, E3)
Mediterranean €€€
Tucked away down a side street from the old city's main leisure areas, the ambience here is as delightful as the food. The menu, always creative, varies according to the rhythm of the seasons. One constant is the excellent rice dishes, especially rice with lobster.
☎ 96 391 38 15 ✉ Calle Boix 6 🕙 lunch Mon-Fri,

dinner Mon-Sat 🚌 2, 5, 16, 28, 80 ♿ good

Dukala (2, B2)
Moroccan €€
Dukala (du *ka* la) is hyperfriendly, intimate (reservations are essential) and bedecked with striped Moroccan fabric. Noreddine prepares the best Maghrabi cuisine in town, including the tastiest of bread rolls. Order a pot of mint tea, poured from a height, or choose from the small, carefully selected wine list.
☎ 96 392 62 53 ✉ Calle Sogueros 5 🕙 lunch Fri-Sun, dinner Tue-Sun 🚌 5, 5B, 27, 80, 95 ♿ fair

El Molinón (2, B3)
Tapas €
El Molinón, all stone and slate, has fat hams cradled on the bar and around 50

THE TAPA
Tradition tells that King Alfonso X (r 1252–84), known as Il Sabio (The Wise), introduced this excellent custom. Aware of the effect of alcohol upon an empty stomach, he decreed that no wine should be served without food. So tavern owners adopted the tradition of serving a modest portion of ham, chorizo or cheese. The small plate would be placed on top of the glass or carafe to *tapar* (cover) it and keep out dust and other alien material. Hence, today's tapa…

MENÚ DEL DÍA

Midweek, it's worth planning your day around a mid-day *menú* (set menu). From Monday to Friday, nearly all restaurants offer a three-course special that may or may not include coffee, wine or both. Whatever the category of the restaurant, *menús del día* are normally an excellent deal. They also let you sample the cuisine of restaurants that otherwise might be above your budgetary limit. Two *menús del día* that offer exceptional value (at €15) are those of La Lola (p51) and Seu-Xerea (p52).

kinds of tapas. The wines are fine but you really ought to invest in a bottle of scrumpy cider from Asturias, in Spain's northwest. Poured from a height, it's a spectacle as well as a drink.

☎ 96 391 15 38 ⊠ Calle Bolsería 40 ☯ lunch & dinner ➌ 5B, 7, 81 ♿ good

La Carmé (2, B3)
Mediterranean €€
La Carmé's *menú* (set menu) – and they keep things simple and only do a set meal (€18) – has scarcely changed in the last 20 years. Why should it when, with its pleasing décor of wood and bare brick, and friendly service, the place offers such superb value?

☎ 96 392 25 32 ⊠ Plaza Mosén Sorell s/n ☯ dinner Mon-Sat ➌ 5, 5B, 27, 80, 95 ♿ fair

La Lluna (2, B2)
Vegetarian €€
La Lluna has been serving quality, reasonably priced vegetarian fare for over 25 years. On two floors, and with walls elaborately tiled, it offers lots of choice (try the cheese-and-carrot cake for dessert) plus daily

specials (go for the seaweed salad if it's on).

☎ 96 392 21 46 ⊠ Calle San Ramón 23 ☯ lunch & dinner Mon-Sat ➌ 5, 28, 80, 95 ♿ fair Ⓥ

La Sucursal (2, B2)
Mediterranean €€€€
La Sucursal, the restaurant of Instituto Valenciano de Arte Moderno (IVAM; p12), is appropriately contemporary – all muted greys and blacks, subtly illuminated. Its fish is of the freshest, and the wine list a veritable book (abstainers can choose from over 30 different mineral waters!). The *menú degustación* (€55) is sheer delight to linger over.

☎ 96 374 66 65 ⊠ Calle Guillem de Castro 118 ☯ lunch Mon-Fri, dinner Mon-Sat ➌ 5, 28, 80, 95 ♿ fair

La Taberna de Marisa (2, C3)
Tapas €€
Choose the intimate upstairs dining area or busy bar, where fat hams hang beside giant crusty loaves of bread. It's not cheap but the ingredients and wines (see the selection of the week chalked on the giant

slateboard) are all prime quality. The *morcilla de Burgos* (roundels of black pudding) is sublime.

☎ 96 392 18 27 ⊠ Calle Caballeros 47 ☯ 1pm-1.30am Mon-Fri, 8pm-1.30am Sat ➌ 5B ♿ fair

La Tastaolletes (2, B2)
Vegetarian €
This tiny place does a creative range of vegetable tapas. Pleasantly informal, it's worth visiting for the friendly atmosphere and good, wholesome food created from quality prime ingredients. There's a good *menú* (€8), the salads are frondy, and the cheesecake with stewed fruits a dream.

☎ 96 392 18 62 ⊠ Calle Salvador Giner 6 ☯ lunch Tue-Sat, dinner Mon-Sat ➌ 5, 28, 80, 95 ♿ good ♿ Ⓥ

Mattilde (2, C2)
Mediterranean €€
At this laid-back, relatively new restaurant, the décor is stylish, modern and unpretentious and the cheery young team offers friendly service. An imaginative à la carte selection and a particularly good-value lunch *menú* are on offer.

☎ 96 382 31 68 ✉ Calle
Roteros 21 ☼ lunch Mon-
Fri, dinner Mon-Sat 🚌 5, 5B,
28, 80, 95 ♿ good

Orient Xpress (2, C2)
Oriental €
Valencia's first noodle bar
was one of the city's first
eateries to opt for a
complete no-smoking policy.
You sit at long wooden
tables, where your menu,
which is also your placemat,
offers reasonably priced
Japanese, Thai and Malay
specialities and great
fruit juices.
☎ 96 306 51 16 💻 www
.orientxpress.info in Spanish
✉ Calle Roteros 12
☼ noon–midnight 🚌 2, 5,
5B, 80, 95 ♿ good 🚲 Ⓥ

Patl Pineda (2, C2)
Mediterranean €
Within the Palacio Pineda
(these days university
premises), this cooperative
offers a superb value
creative lunchtime *menú*
(€8) that's a favourite with
valencaons in the know. It's
open to all; go through the
main door and head for the
lone palm tree that spreads
its shade over the rear patio.
☎ 96 391 22 62 ✉ Plaza
del Carmen 4 ☼ lunch

Burdeos In Love has an enormous range of Spanish red...

Mon–Fri Sep-Jul 🚌 2, 5, 5B,
80, 95 ♿ good

Suchi Cru 96 (2, B3)
Japanese €€
It's sushi and only sushi at
this intimate place with
barely 20 places. Eat at the
bar and you can watch the
deft way the staff slice
and pat the subtle morsels,
all prepared fresh and on
the spot.
☎ 96 392 54 92 ✉ Calle
Pintor Zariñena 3 ☼ lunch &
dinner 🚌 5, 7, 81 ♿ fair

HORCHATA
This sweet, opaque, very Valencian drink is made
from pressed *chufas* (tiger nuts), into which you dip
large finger-shaped buns called *fartons;* both name
and taste are to savour. Two traditional places to sample this drink in the heart of town are **Horchatería
de Santa Catalina** (2, C4; ☎ 96 391 23 79; Plaza
Santa Catalina 6; ☼ 9am-10pm) and **Horchatería
el Siglo** (2, C4; ☎ 96 391 84 66; Plaza Santa Catalina
6; ☼ 8am-9pm Sun-Fri).

ELSEWHERE IN CENTRO HISTÓRICO

Bodegó de la Sarieta
(2, C3)
Mediterranean €€
Tiled, its walls covered in
prints and posters, this
smallish, very *valenciano*
place does a great range of
tapas, rich in local specialities
(ask for the menu in English).
Mains too are varied and
inventive and there's an
excellent *menú* (€14) with
plenty of choice.
☎ 96 392 35 38 ✉ Calle
Juristas 4 ☼ lunch & dinner
Mon-Sat 🚌 4, 6, 8, 70, 71
♿ fair

Burdeos in Love (2, D4)
Mediterranean €€€
Art Nouveau lamps hang
beneath the ornately stuc-
coed ceiling of this smart
restaurant with its modern
clean-lined décor. Both the
midday *menú* (€16) and the

menú degustación (€36) are excellent value and there's an impressive wine list, especially of Spanish reds. Mineral water, however, at €5 is overpriced, even though it's travelled from Wales... ☎ 96 391 43 50 ✉ Calle Mar 4 🕒 lunch Mon-Sat, dinner Mon-Fri 🚌 4, 6, 8, 70, 71 ♿ good Ⓥ

Cardamom (2, B4)
Mediterranean €€
With bags of space, comfortable leather seating and the wackiest of wall clocks, Cardamon is a fashionable restaurant in an unfashionable area. Everything is sure-footed, from the tableware to the careful presentation of the food to the stylish artwork. The lunchtime *menú* (€10.50, including a glass of excellent house wine) is exceptional value. ☎ 96 391 00 19 ✉ Plaza Don Juan de Villarrasa 6 🕒 lunch Mon-Fri, dinner Tue-Sat 🚌 7, 60, 81 ♿ good 🚼

Casa Dodo (2, B3)
Mediterranean €€
Run by Mum, darting in and out of the kitchen, and her son and daughter, Casa Dodo's times are restricted but may expand (do ring to confirm). With only 20 places, and its niches full of family mementos, this place is hyperfriendly; Chantal, daughter of the house, happily pulls up a chair to explain the creative menu in English. ☎ 96 391 07 70 ✉ Calle Carda 6 🕒 dinner from 9.30pm Thu-Sat 🚌 7, 60, 81 ♿ good

Cien Montaditos (2, D3)
Tapas €
You've a choice of 100 fillings (all €1) for your *montadito* (miniroll). Fill in the order form at your table, choose a drink, present it at the counter and listen for your name to be called. Speedy and superb value, though they don't accept reservations. ☎ 902 197494 ✉ Plaza de la Reina 10 🕒 10.30am-midnight 🚌 4, 6, 8, 70, 71 ♿ good

Commo (2, D5)
Mediterranean €€€
The décor at this classy restaurant is minimalist, uncluttered and bathed in cool blue light. The menu changes regularly and radically as the seasons succeed each other. Everything, including the ice

NEVER ON A MONDAY
Never's a tad too strong but Monday isn't the best day for fish dishes. The local fishing boats don't put out on Sundays so what's on the menu has been in the fridge over the weekend or comes fresh plucked from the deep freeze.

cream, is confected on the premises from the freshest of ingredients.

☎ 96 352 36 49 ✉ Calle Pascual y Genís 3 ☾ lunch Mon-Sat, dinner Tue-Sat 🚌 5, 6, 35, 62, 81 ♿ good

Enbandeja (2, C5)
Self-service €
Brightly painted and cheerful, this relaxed self-service place is a favourite with local office workers. It does great-value continental breakfasts (€2.50) and lunches (€8.40 including a drink and coffee). If you're especially hungry, you can order two mains rather than a starter and main.

☎ 96 394 06 95 ✉ Calle San Vicente Mártir 24 ☾ 8.30am–9pm Mon-Fri, 1.30-4pm Sat Oct-May, 9am–9pm Mon-Fri Jun-Sep 🚌 4, 6, 8, 10, 36 ♿ fair ♿

FrescCo (2, D6)
Self-service €
FrescCo's all-you-can-eat under-€10 buffet offers a veritable kitchen garden of salad items and a choice of pasta or pizza. With its bare, mellow brickwork, it's an agreeable place to dine in, though you're not encouraged to linger once dessert's over. Also at Calle Salamanca 6 (3, D3; ☎ 96 119 91 39).

☎ 96 310 63 88 ✉ Calle Felix Pizcueta 6 ☾ 12.30pm-1am 🚌 5, 6, 10, 32, 81 ♿ fair ♿

La Lola (2, C3)
Spanish Nouvelle Cuisine €€€
Up an alley beside the cathedral, here's a very suave number indeed, where white bar, walls and furnishings contrast with stark reds,

Just dotty about La Lola

blacks and giant polka dots. Cool jazz trills. Desserts such as creamed white chocolate, raspberry delight, gooey Greek yoghurt, pistachio and crunchy biscuit (oh yes, that's all one dish) are wickedly tempting.

☎ 96 391 80 45 🖥 www .lalolarestaurante.com ✉ Subida del Toledano 8 ☾ lunch & dinner Tue-Sat 🚌 4, 11, 16, 28, 71 ♿ fair

La Pappardella (2, C3)
Italian €€
La Pappardella, with its ultrafriendly, speedy staff, is a popular haunt of younger diners. Built on two floors around a central patio, it's agreeably broken up into smaller areas and has a small street terrace. The cuisine is authentically Italian and reasonably priced.

☎ 96 391 89 15 ✉ Calle Bordadores 5 ☾ lunch & dinner 🚌 4, 6, 8, 70, 71 ♿ fair ♿

La Utielana (2, D5)
Valencian €
Tucked away off Calle Prócida and not easy to track down, La Utielana well merits a minute or two of sleuthing. Clad in blue-and-white tiling and very Valencian, it packs in the lunchtime crowds, drawn by the wholesome fare and exceptional value for money. Arrive early as it doesn't take reservations.

☎ 96 352 94 14 ✉ Plaza Picadero dos Aguas 3 ☾ lunch Mon-Sat, dinner Mon-Fri 🚌 4, 6, 8, 19, 36 ♿ fair

Les Níts (2, A4)
Mediterranean €€€
Intimate with minimalist décor, The Nights is a welcome newcomer to Valencia's expanding roll call of quality, modern restaurants. It offers a splendid six-course *menú* (€21) and tantalising à la carte choices. Portions don't spill over the edge of the

plate but the quality is excellent and the imaginative desserts to die for.

☎ 96 391 63 40 ✉ Calle Botánico 12 ⏱ lunch & dinner Tue-Sat 🚌 2, 60, 61, 62, 63 Ⓜ Turia ♿ good

Neco (2, D5)
Self-service €

Another great central self-service choice is Neco. The buffet (€9 Monday to Friday, €11.75 Saturday and Sunday) is rich in salads and has plenty of options for vegetarians. There's also a special price for children. There are branches at Avenida Aragón 25 (3, D2) and Centro Comercial El Saler (3, E4).

☎ 96 369 55 21 ✉ Calle Pascual y Genís 9 ⏱ lunch & dinner 🚌 5, 6, 14, 62, 81 ♿ good 🚼

Palacio de la Bellota
(2, D6)
Seafood €€€€

Palacio de la Bellota is one of a cluster of superb upmarket seafood restaurants flanking this narrow, pedestrianised street. Shellfish are hauled fresh from the Mediterranean and the fish selection too is excellent. There's ham as well, with legs of it hanging in profusion from the ceiling. Eat inside or on the street terrace.

☎ 96 351 53 61 ✉ Calle Mosén Femades 7 ⏱ lunch & dinner Mon-Sat 🚌 5, 6, 10, 15, 81 ♿ good

Sagardí (2, C4)
Basque €-€€€

Enjoy delightful tapas (€1.20 each) downstairs at this quality Basque café-restaurant. Keep the sticks that impale them since that's

how they tot up your bill. Try the white Basque Txakoli wine or a glass of Sidra de Astigarraga, cider from the Basque country. Upstairs is the even more impressive restaurant.

☎ 96 391 06 68 ✉ Calle San Vicente Mártir 6 ⏱ 9am-12.30am 🚌 4, 6, 8, 17, 19 ♿ fair

Seu-Xerea (2, D3)
Mediterranean Fusion €€€

This smart, welcoming restaurant is favourably quoted in almost every English-language press article about Valencia. Its creative, regularly changing à la carte menu features dishes both international and rooted in Spain. It does a warmly recommended *menú del día* (€15). Wines, selected by the chef-owner, a qualified sommelier, are uniformly excellent.

☎ 96 392 40 00 🖥 www .seuxerea.com ✉ Calle Conde Almodóvar 4 ⏱ lunch & dinner Mon-Sat 🚌 4, 6, 8, 70, 71 ♿ good

Shiraz (2, B3)
Mediterranean €€

Named after the grape varietal, Shiraz indeed carries a good wine list. A satisfyingly small restaurant, its décor is tasteful and 21st century. Salads are a delight and there's plenty of choice for vegetarians. Service could be jollier but what comes from the kitchen is creative, using the freshest of ingredients.

☎ 96 391 03 64 ✉ Calle Conquista 3 ⏱ lunch & dinner Mon-Sat 🚌 5B, 7, 81 ♿ good

Tapinería (2, C4)
Mediterranean €€

This intimate, split-level place is broken up into small niches. Upstairs has more atmosphere but can become fearsomely hot in summer. That's when the rear terrace, on a quiet pedestrianised square, comes into its own. There's no à la carte selection but the innovative set menu (€18) offers plenty of choice.

☎ 96 391 54 40 ⊠ Calle Tapinería 16 🕑 dinner Mon-Sat 🚌 4, 6, 8, 70, 71 ♿ fair

Tasca Ángel (2, C3)
Tapas €

If the sound and scent of fresh, boned sardines sizzling on the griddle drives you wild, call by Tasca Ángel, 60 years in business, scarcely more than a hole in the wall and something of a Valencian institution. Help them down with a glass of chilled white wine.

☎ 96 391 78 35 ⊠ Calle Purísima 2 🕑 lunch & dinner Mon-Sat 🚌 7, 27, 28, 81 ♿ fair

Tasca Jesús (2, B6)
Valencian €€

Sides of ham like sumo wrestlers' legs festoon the walls of this popular restaurant. What's on depends upon what's freshest in the market that day. The superb midday *menú* costs €10 in the bar, €14 (including mellow organic wine) in the restaurant.

☎ 96 351 13 22 ⊠ Calle Jesús 22 🕑 lunch Mon-Fri, dinner Mon-Sat 🚌 9, 10, 17, 27, 71 ♿ fair 🚭

L'EIXAMPLE & RUSSAFA

Alghero (3, D3)
Mediterranean Italian €€€

Alghero, where everything is attractively presented and mouth-watering, offers essentially Mediterranean cuisine with a strong Italian overlay. Try, in particular, the rice dishes (for a minimum of two) and fish, then indulge in one of the waist-enhancing desserts.

☎ 96 333 35 79 ⊠ Calle Burriana 52 🕑 lunch & dinner Tue-Sat 🚌 1, 2, 79, 80, 95 ♿ good

Ángel Azul (2, F6)
Spanish €€€€

One of the first of Valencia's truly gourmet restaurants, the Blue Angel, in business for just over 10 years, has spawned chefs who have later made their reputations elsewhere in Valencia. Its secret is prime quality ingredients, such as free-range poultry or organic vegetables, all, wherever possible, locally produced.

☎ 96 374 56 56 💻 www .angelazul.com in Spanish ⊠ Calle Conde de Altea 33 🕑 lunch & dinner Tue-Sat 🚌 1, 2, 3, 79, 80 ♿ good

Assaggi (2, F6)
Italian €€

Small, minimalist and with attractive stainless-steel furniture, Assaggi, run by an engaging young team, does an excellent-value lunch *menú* (€10.50). Beware the house tiramisu, so

GREAT HOTEL DINING

Several upmarket Valencian hotels have excellent gastronomic restaurants that are open to all-comers. You'll eat very well indeed at Ampar, the restaurant of Palau de la Mar (p70), with its excellent wine list and five-course *menú degustación* (€55). Other hotels with restaurants that merit a visit for their own sake include Neptuno (pictured, p70), Ad Hoc (p71) and Puerta Valencia (p70).

wonderfully melt-in-the-mouth that you may pass out.

☎ 96 344 01 75 ✉ Calle Conde de Altea 26 ☯ lunch & dinner Mon-Sat 🚌 1, 2, 3, 79, 80 ♿ good

Beirut (2, F6)

Middle Eastern €€
Adorned with blown-up photos of old Beirut, here's a little corner of the Levant on Spain's Levante coast. Go for the 10-dish mezze (€15) or choose à la carte, then relax over coffee with a hubble bubble. A belly dancer adds extra spice to the cuisine at 10.30pm, Wednesday to Saturday.

☎ 96 374 59 05 ✉ Calle Conde de Altea 39 ☯ lunch & dinner Tue-Sun 🚌 1, 2, 79, 80, 95 ♿ good ☗

Casa Botella (3, C3)

Mediterranean €€
This delightfully friendly, intimate place is run by an enthusiastic young team. The menu veers towards fusion – how about *albondigas al curry* (Spanish meatballs in a curry sauce) for a meeting of culinary cultures? Ask for Les

Alcusses, a very palatable red wine (€12) from the genial owner's home village.

☎ 654 849333 ✉ Calle Pintor Salvador Abril 28 ☯ lunch & dinner Tue-Sat 🚌 6, 14, 15, 19, 40 ♿ good

Casa Juan (3, C3)

Mediterranean €€€
The owner buys fish fresh from the local market, a mere 50m away. They're prepared simply, with no messing about, and retaining all their juices. When we visited, a grizzled old fisherman entered with a bucketful, some still flopping, that

were immediately added to the day's offers. Dedicated carnivores should sink their teeth into a thick ox steak.

☎ 96 374 04 24 ✉ Calle Donoso Cortes 8 ☯ lunch Mon-Sun, dinner Mon-Sat 🚌 6, 14, 15, 19, 40 ♿ good

Casa Roberto (3, C3)

Valencian €€€
It styles itself as La Boutique del Arroz (The Rice Boutique), and with good reason. With a dozen or more rice dishes (they've even created a topical new one – *arroz Copa América!*), it's about the best restaurant in town to sample this typical Valencian product and also does excellent grilled meat and fish.

☎ 96 395 13 61 🖥 www .boutiquedelarroz.com in Spanish ✉ Calle Maestro Gozalbo 19 ☯ lunch Tue-Sun, dinner Tue-Sat 🚌 1, 3, 41, 79, 80 ♿ good ☗

Che (3, C3)

Basque €
Divided into intimate little booths, this popular Basque place, its walls plastered with photos, watercolours and whatever takes the owner's

fancy, is full of character. Over 50 years in business, it offers excellent value (particularly the midday *menú* at €6.20) and friendly service.
☎ 96 374 65 25 ✉ Avenida Antiguo Reino de Valencia 9 🕙 lunch Tue-Sun, dinner Tue-Fri 🚍 1, 2, 3, 79, 80 🚹 good 🚹

Cinquante Cinq (3, D3)
French €€
Run by an enterprising Englishman with a Scot and an Argentinian powering the kitchen and a French maître, this place breathes entente cordiale. The inventive menu changes regularly and the carefully selected wine list has a good representation from north of the Pyrenees.
☎ 96 325 50 29 ✉ Calle Joaquin Costa 55 🕙 lunch daily, dinner Tue-Sat 🚍 1, 2, 3, 79, 80 🚹 good 🚹

El Gaucho (2, F6)
Argentinian €€
You're here strictly for the meat – hunky slabs of prime beef, cooked the way only Argentinians can. The weight of each dish is indicated on the menu so you know exactly what's sizzling away for you.
☎ 96 395 20 17 ✉ Calle Conde de Altea 51 🕙 lunch Sun, dinner daily 🚍 1, 2, 3, 79, 80 🚹 good

El México de María (3, C3)
Mexican €€
Valencia has its share of *soi-disant* Mexican restaurants. For authentic cuisine, just as you'd find it south of the Río Grande and with no concessions to Tex-Mex or European palates, head

Stylish Riff (p56)

for this small place in Russafa, controlled back-stage by jolly, round María in the kitchen.
☎ 96 332 80 78 ✉ Calle Denia 20 🕙 lunch & dinner Tue-Sun 🚍 1, 2, 3, 79, 80 🚹 good 🚹

Jalasan (3, D3)
Korean €€
Myung Keun Lee not only serves authentic, tasty Korean food (the menu's in English too). He's also a gifted photographer. His haunting black-and-white photos bedeck the walls of this attractive, dark-wood place, where classical music throbs softly in the background.
☎ 96 333 72 07 ✉ Calle Ciscar 43 🕙 lunch Tue-Sun, dinner Tue-Sat 🚍 1, 2, 12, 79, 80 🚹 fair

La Estancia (3, C3)
Argentinian €€
Here's a place for seriously dedicated carnivores. Begin with an *empanada* (Argentinian pastie) before choosing from the magnificent beef selection. The menu specifies whether a dish is from the Argentinian pampas or locally reared. The too modestly named Baby Bife, weighing in at 375g, will tax the most determined trencherperson.
☎ 96 316 12 70 ✉ Calle Maestro Gozalbo 15 🕙 lunch & dinner Tue-Sun 🚍 1, 2, 3, 79, 80 🚹 good 🚹

Mey Mey (2, A6)
Chinese €€
Nibble delicate dim sums, followed by the *fantasía Mandarín* (shrimps, mixed meats and vegetables in

an edible basket of crispy noodles). The low ceiling of this very superior Cantonese restaurant exudes positive feng shui, despite the pair of decidedly kitsch herons, spewing water into a central pool.

☎ 96 384 07 47 ✉ Calle Historiador Diago 19 ⏰ lunch & dinner Sep-Jul 🚌 1, 2, 3, 79, 80 Ⓜ Plaça d'Espanya ♿ fair

Riff (3, C3)
Mediterranean €€€€

Riff is as satisfyingly spare in design as any Japanese equivalent. Chef Bernd Knöller imaginatively prepares the finest Mediterranean ingredients, supplemented with delicate titbits that keep rolling in. The lunch *menú* (€20) is great value. For €10 more, each of its three courses comes accompanied by a specially selected wine.

☎ 96 333 53 53 🖥 www .restaurante-riff.com in Spanish ✉ Calle Conde de Altea 18 ⏰ lunch & dinner

Tue-Sat 🚌 1, 2, 3, 79, 80 🅿 ♿ good

Villaplana (3, B2)
Tapas €€

Villaplana is a long-established favourite for a night of tapas nibbling. Even though Villaplana can accommodate 350 (how is a mystery since you never feel overcrowded), it's wise to reserve for dinner. 'We specialise in everything' says the tongue-in-cheek business card and, indeed, the range of dishes on offer is huge.

☎ 96 385 06 13 ✉ Calle Doctor Sanchis Sivera 24 ⏰ 8am-midnight Mon-Sat Ⓜ Ángel Guimerá ♿ good 🚱 Ⓥ

NORTH OF JARDINES DEL TURIA

Amado Mío (3, D2)
Mediterranean €€

Large and pleasantly minimalist in design, My

Beloved opens at 8pm to catch the after-office trade. Its à la carte list is slim but creative with four fish and four meat/poultry choices. The twee toilet signing might throw you: *Mía* is hers, *Mío* for him!

☎ 96 393 09 68 🖥 www .amadomio.net in Spanish ✉ Calle Bélgica 30 ⏰ lunch Mon-Fri, dinner Mon-Sat 🚌 18, 41, 81, 89, 90 ♿ good

Casa Clemencia (3, D1)
Valencian €€

A café throughout the day and popular lunch and dinner venue, Casa Clemencia, its walls decorated with old agricultural implements, does paella in the traditional way, over orange-wood fires that blaze in the rear. The unforgettable signature dessert *naranja quemada* is a delicious orange-based confection.

☎ 96 360 10 01 ✉ Avenida Primado Reig 179 ⏰ 8am-11pm 🚌 31, 89, 90 ♿ fair 🚱

El Salado (3, D2)

Mediterranean/French €€
A typical corner café by day, serving constantly fresh tapas, El Salado offers an enticing lunchtime *menú* (€10). At night it goes Gallic, with a short, creative, French-oriented à la carte selection.
☎ 96 369 84 04 ✉ Calle Polo y Peyrolón ☽ lunch & dinner Mon-Sat ⊟ 18, 89, 90

Restaurante Antonio Alba (3, D2)

Mediterranean €€€
This elegant, welcoming restaurant, right in front of the football stadium, is famous for its reliable Mediterranean cuisine, especially the hearty meat dishes, and also for the sheer variety of its rice dishes, simmered to perfection.
☎ 96 361 93 65 ✉ Avenida Aragón 40 ☽ lunch & dinner ⊟ 18, 89, 90 ♿ good

Tastem (3, D2)

Japanese €€€
Tastem was designed with great contemporary flair by a young *valenciano* who's spent many years in Japan. The décor, all beige and soft greys, is positively soothing, as a pair of Japanese chefs chop and

Fancy a late-night snack of *churros* and *bunelos*?

mould the subtlest of dishes behind the long counter
☎ 96 369 68 51 ▢ www .tastem.com ✉ Calle Ernesto Ferrer 14 ☽ lunch Tue-Fri, dinner Tue-Sat ⊟ 18, 89, 90 ♿ good

PORT, LAS ARENAS & LA MALVARROSA

Bodega Montaña (4, A3)

Tapas €€
Serving excellent wines (well, the owner is a qualified sommelier) and varied tapas (just try the fresh anchovies) since 1836, Bodega Montaña, with its marble bar, barrels and yellowing posters, is a Valencian institution. It's our favourite place in all Valencia. Take your chance at the crowded bar or reserve one of the few interior tables – and don't tell them we suggested you come here.
☎ 96 367 23 14 ✉ Calle José Benlliure 69 ☽ lunch Mon-Sun, dinner Mon-Sat ⊟ 1, 2, 32, in summer 20, 22, 23 ♿ fair

WORTH A TRIP

Restaurante Submarino (3, E4; ☎ 96 197 55 65; Camino de las Moreras s/n; ☽ lunch & dinner; bus 13, 15, 19, 35, 40, 95) is an elegant circular restaurant, its broad, glowing lamps like giant lily pads, within the Oceanogràfic (p10). Instead of wallpaper, over a thousand silvery bream and sardines slowly gyrate. If you feel uncomfortable eating fish as those unblinking eyes stare reproachfully, there are meat alternatives… The cuisine's mainly Mediterranean, and, with all those fishy mouths to feed, it doesn't come cheap. Parking is available at Museo de las Ciencias, and there is good lift access to the restaurant.

Casa Navarro
Valencian €€
Dearer than the Las Arenas restaurants, Casa Navarro is best approached on foot, along the promenade, to work up an appetite. Occupying an old seaside villa, it specialises in rice dishes. Choose the large interior, glassed-in patio or open terrace enjoying the sea breezes.
☎ 96 372 00 27 ⊠ Avenida Mare Nostrum 141 ⏲ lunch & dinner Wed-Mon Jun-Sep, lunch Sun, Mon, Wed-Sat, dinner Fri & Sat Oct-May 🚌 1, 2, in summer 20, 22, 23 Ⓟ ♿ fair ⚹

De Tot un Poc (4, A3)
Tapas €€
This tiny restaurant has only five tables. Neat as a new pin, this is one of several great tapas places in the narrow streets of Cabanyal. If they're in season, do order the *almejas y alcachofas* (€8.40) – clams, artichokes and a delightful blend of sea and land.
☎ 96 367 11 68 ⊠ Calle Barraca 28 ⏲ lunch &

dinner Mon-Fri mid-Mar–mid-Sep, lunch Mon-Sat, dinner Thu-Sat mid-Sep–mid-Mar 🚌 1, 2, 32, in summer 20, 22, 23 ♿ good

El Polp (4, A3)
Tapas €
The Octopus, an informal place where local artists exhibit around the walls, pulls in a great social mix. It has an inventive midday *menú* (€10). At night it serves tasty fish and seafood tapas, which are chalked up on the blackboard beside the entrance.
☎ 96 355 72 73 ⊠ Calle Reina 148 ⏲ lunch Mon-Sat, dinner Mon-Sat 🚌 1, 2, in summer 20, 22, 23 ♿ good ⚹

La Pepica (4, A3)
Valencian €€
Larger and more expensive than its competitors, and renowned for its rice dishes and seafood, this is where Ernest Hemingway, among many other luminaries, once strutted. Between courses, browse through the photos and

tributes (from prominent and not-so-prominent clients) that plaster the walls, and see how many you recognise.
☎ 96 371 03 66 🖥 www .lapepica.com in Spanish ⊠ Paseo de Neptuno 6-8 ⏲ lunch Mon-Sun, dinner Mon-Sat 🚌 1, 2, in summer 20, 22, 23 🚋 Las Arenas ♿ excellent ⚹

Lonja del Pescado Frito (4, A2)
Valencian €€
One block back from the beach at La Malvarrosa and right beside the tram stop, this busy but informal place in what's little more than an adorned tin shack offers unbeatable value for fresh fish. So grab an order form as you enter and fill it in at your table.
☎ 96 355 35 35 ⊠ Calle Eugenia Viñes 243 ⏲ lunch Sat & Sun, dinner Tue-Sun Mar-Oct, lunch & dinner Sat & Sun Nov-Feb 🚌 1, 2 in summer 20, 22, 23 🚋 Eugenia Viñes ♿ good ⚹

Entertainment

Fuelled by a large student population, Valencia has one of Spain's best nightlife scenes. It cranks up late; most bars and pubs begin to fill around 10pm but the majority of dance clubs don't deign to open their doors until midnight at the earliest.

The Barrio del Carmen, with both the grungiest and grooviest collection of bars, has by far the best vibes. Around the old university, in and around Avenidas Aragón and Blasco Ibañez, bars and dance clubs swarm with students. The streets east of Gran Vía Marqués del Turia, and extending into Russafa, are an up-and-coming area, rich in bars and restaurants, while those around the Mercado de Abastos attract a younger set, eager for through-the-night action.

There are plenty of resources for keeping abreast of what's on. *La Turia* and *Que y Donde* are weekly guides on sale at kiosks and newsagents. *Hello Valencia* and *24-7 Valencia* are free monthlies available in tourist offices and selected bars and clubs. *Cool Carmen* has informed tip-offs about worthwhile places within Barrio del Carmen. Check the website of **Thisisvalencia Mapazine** (www.thisisvalencia.com) for greater detail.

To book tickets for major events call **Servientrada** (☎ 902 115577) or the **Corte Inglés department store** (☎ 902 400222), which has ticket offices at its stores on Calle Colón (2, E5) and in the Nuevo Centro (3, B1).

It's a city littered with bars with character – in more ways than one!

BARS & PUBS

Backstage Russafa (3, C3)
Lively Backstage is popular with theatre folk and hangers on – hence the name, décor and theatrical lighting. Cocktails are shaken with histrionic panache and even the toilets are labelled (oh dear me, yes) *actores* and *actrices*.
☎ 96 334 89 13 ✉ Calle Literato Azorín 1 ⏰ from 7pm 🚌 7, 8

Bar Manolo el del Bombo (3, D2)
You already know Manolo if you've ever seen the Spanish national football team play. With a beret bigger than a dinner plate, he thumps his base drum – there it is, dangling from the ceiling – to rouse the fans. His bar (appropriately, in the shadow of Valencia's raked stadium) is plastered with photos and mementos.
☎ 96 393 04 60 💻 www .manoloeldelbombo.com in Spanish ✉ Plaza del Valencia Club de Fútbol 5 ⏰ 7.30am-2am Tue-Sun Ⓜ Aragón

Classy but cluttered Café Infanta

Outdoors is the place to be at Café Lisboa

Cafe-Bar Negrito (2, C3)
The crowd and music spill out onto a large pedestrianised square. This local favourite traditionally attracts an intellectual, left-wing crowd. You'll be lucky to find a seat after around 9pm.
☎ 96 391 42 33 ✉ Plaza del Negrito ⏰ 3pm-3.30am 🚌 4, 6, 28, 36, 70 ♿ fair

Café de las Horas (2, D3)
High Baroque, laid-back, tapestries, candelabras dripping wax and quality recorded music of all genres: such a setting demands a special drink. An exotic cocktail? Or pick from the impressive list of local brandies and sparkling wines. If all that incense brings on the sneezes, opt for the street terrace.
☎ 96 391 73 36 ✉ Calle Conde Almodóvar 1 ⏰ 4pm-1.30am Sun-Wed, 4pm-2.30am Thu-Sat 🚌 2, 6, 8, 80, 95 ♿ fair

Café Infanta (2, B3)
Café Infanta is one of a cluster of enticing choices in and around Plaza del Tossal. Good for a terrace drink (look first – this side

of the otherwise respectable square is favoured by dossers and drunks), its interior is a clutter of cinema memorabilia, display cases, publicity photos and posters.
☎ 96 392 16 23 ✉ Plaza del Tossal 3 ⏰ 7pm-2.30am 🚌 5B, 7, 81 ♿ fair

Café Lisboa (2, C4)
This lively, student-oriented bar mounts temporary painting exhibitions. Its innards are a bit cramped and constricting; the large, street-side terrace is the place to sip your drink. The bulletin board is a palimpsest of small ads for apartment shares and language tuition.
☎ 96 391 94 84 ✉ Plaza Doctor Collado 9 ⏰ 9am-2.30am 🚌 7, 27, 28, 81 ♿ fair

Fox Congo (2, C3)
Haunt of Valencia's beautiful people, trendy Fox Congo has a cool, back-lit alabaster bar split by a giant globe and walls clad in leather and sheet-metal. More? Well, men pee against a glass wall protecting bushy hydrangeas and exotic

SPECIAL EVENTS

January
Día de los Reyes Magos (6 January)
The Three Kings lead a street cavalcade
and children traditionally receive
presents.

March
Las Fallas (15–19 March) See p62 for
full details.
Semana Santa (March–April) Elaborate
Holy Week processions in the district of
La Malvarrosa.
Fiesta de San Vicente Ferrer (1st
Sunday after Easter) Colourful parades
and miracle plays celebrate the wondrous
miracles of this local saint.

April
Mostra de Vins, Caves i Licors (Five
days in early April) A festival of local food
and wine in the Jardines del Turia, south
of Puente de la Exposición.

May
Fiesta de la Virgen (2nd Sunday) The
effigy of the Virgen de los Desamparados,
hemmed in by fervent believers, makes
the short journey across Plaza de la Virgen
to the cathedral.

June
Corpus Christi (9th Sunday after Easter)
Celebrated with an elaborate procession
and mystery plays.
Día de San Juan (Misummer's Day; 23–24
June) Thousands mark the longest day,
with night-time bonfires on the beach.

July
Feria de Julio (2nd half of July)
Performing arts, brass-band competitions,
bullfights, a jazz festival, fireworks and
a 'battle of the flowers' in Paseo de la
Alameda.

October
Día de la Comunidad (9 October)
Commemorates the city's 1238 liberation
from the Arabs with processions and
elaborate Moros y Cristianos (Moors and
Christians) parades.
Festival of Mediterranean Cinema
A whole week of films from around the
Mediterranean.
Valencia Bienial (October–November)
Every two years (the 4th edition is
scheduled for 2007), Valencia hosts this
festival of modern visual arts.

LAS FALLAS

Las Fallas, Europe's largest street party, is an exuberant, round-the-clock swirl of fireworks, music, explosions and fire. This wild fiesta honours San José (St Joseph), father of Jesus. Its origins, says tradition, go back to the time when carpenters' apprentices, once spring was in the air, burnt winter's accumulated cut-offs and shavings in the street to honour their patron, the Greatest Carpenter of All.

The *fallas* themselves – more than 350 of them – are huge sculptures of papier-mâché and, increasingly, environmentally harmful polystyrene. Reaching up to 15m in height, the most expensive cost over €120,000 (oh yes, we've got those euro zeros right!). Grotesque, colourful and kitsch, they satirise celebrities, current affairs and local customs.

Round-the-clock festivities include street parties, paella-cooking competitions, parades, open-air concerts, bullfights and nightly free firework displays. Then, just after midnight on 19 March, every single *falla* goes up in flames, except for one small *ninot* (figurine), which is elected by popular vote, and saved for display in the city's Museo Fallero (p23).

grasses (our author, alas, can't speak for the Ladies). ☎ 96 392 55 27 ✉ Calle Caballeros 35 ⏰ 7pm-2.30am Mon-Sat 🚌 5B ♿ fair

San Jaume (2, C3)

The lovely wooden bar was once the counter of this converted pharmacy. There's no room to drink at it but ample space on the outside terrace, ideal for people watching. Alternatively, the 1st floor is all quiet crannies and quaint, poky passageways. ☎ 96 391 24 01 ✉ Calle Caballeros 51 ⏰ noon-1.30am 🚌 5B, 7, 81 ♿ fair

The Lounge (2, C4)

Run by Fiona from Ireland, this friendly bar is a popular haunt of foreign students. There's wi-fi, an Internet terminal and a Monday Spanish-English language interchange. It also does tempting snacks and shakes some mean cocktails. ☎ 96 391 80 94 💻 www .theloungecafebar.com ✉ Calle Purísima s/n

⏰ 10am-1.30am Mon-Fri, 4pm-1.30am Sat & Sun 🚌 7, 27, 28, 81 ♿ good

Turmix (2, B2)

A bar with dancing, Turmix blasts out the best of fringe rock from across the decades. There's one room for chilling out, one for dancing, each clad in psychedelic art work. The beer's not the least of this new arrival's attractions. ✉ Calle Doctor Chiarri 8 ⏰ 11.30pm-3.30am Wed-Sat 🚌 5, 5B, 27, 80, 95

Xino-Xano (2, B3)

Here's a place for connoisseurs of the best in reggae, dub and funk music. The genial owner, a well-known DJ in his own right, picks from his personal collection. Split level, the upstairs part is more intimate though smokier. ☎ 615 989889 ✉ Calle Alta 28 ⏰ 6pm-2am Tue-Sat 🚌 5, 5B, 27, 80, 95

Zumería Naturalia (2, D4)

This semi-basement place serves up juicy, fruity cocktails, with or without an alcoholic kick. Measures are huge, in glasses the size of goldfish bowls. It's popular with couples, sipping

Go outdoors at San Jaume but first check the wooden bar

through straws and gazing deep into each other's eyes. Finding a comfortable posture in the deep wicker chairs is an art in itself.
☎ 96 391 12 11 ✉ Calle del Mar 12 🕒 5pm-2.30am Mon-Wed, Fri & Sat, 5pm-1.15am Thu, 5-10.30pm Sun 🚌 4, 6, 8, 70, 71

LIVE MUSIC

Live it ain't, but for a couple of bars that play the best in music, see p62.

Black Note (3, D2)
Valencia's best and most active jazz venue has live music Monday to Thursday (with an all-comers jam session on Monday). On Friday and Saturday, there's good canned blues, soul and jazz. Admission, including first drink, costs from €6 to €15 depending on who's grooving.
☎ 96 393 36 63 ✉ Calle Polo y Peyrolón 15 🕒 10.30pm-3.30am Mon-Sat 🚌 18, 71, 89, 90 ♿ fair

Café del Duende (2, A2)
Long-established Café del Duende, a little corner of southern Spain, offers quality live, authentic flamenco on Thursday plus some Fridays. Wednesdays are for café-theatre, folk and ethnic music. The place is a small sweatbox so arrive early to be sure of a place.

Chill out at Black Note with great jazz

☎ 630 455289 ✉ Calle Turia 62 🕒 from 11pm Wed-Sat 🚌 5, 7, 81, 95

Cormorán (3, B3)
South of the train station, Cormorán has the pulling power to bring in the big names of pop and rock. Recent acts include Cracker and Sidonie. It has a couple of auditoriums, on two floors, and is only open when there's a gig.
☎ 607 659705 💻 www .cormoran.es in Spanish ✉ Calle San Vicente Mártir 200 🕒 from 9.30pm, concert evenings Ⓜ Jesús ♿ fair

El Loco (2, A5)
Puts on live concerts nightly, often by artists from beyond Spain, from Wednesday to Saturday, and runs house and techno sessions on other nights. Choose your night according to your music then, the concert over, dance on until throwing-out time.
☎ 96 392 26 07 💻 www .lococlub.org in Spanish ✉ Calle Erudito Orellana 12 € €5-15 🚌 3, 70, 72, 79 ♿ fair

Jimmy Glass (2, C3)
Clad with photos of giants of the genre, Jimmy Glass is just what you want from a jazz bar – dim, smoky and serving jumbo measures of creative cocktails. The owner plays the coolest of sounds from his vast CD collection. There's a live combo alternate Tuesdays at 9.30pm (admission €5).
✉ Calle Baja 28 🕒 8pm-2am 🚌 5, 5B, 27, 80, 95 ♿ fair

Creative cocktails and good jazz at Jimmy Glass (p63)

La Linterna (2, C5)

This is a cool, primarily jazz venue where the beautiful people and business crowd come to see and be seen. Tuesday and Wednesday are for jazz and blues, Thursday it's reggae and Latin, Friday pure jazz, while house of the gentler sort prevails on Saturday.

☎ 96 352 01 61 ✉ Calle Linterna 11 ⏰ 7pm-3am Tue-Sat Ⓜ Xàtiva ♿ fair

DANCE CLUBS & DISCOTECAS

Bananas

Go Bananas at the maxiest maxidisco you'll ever party at. On two floors, it packs in dancers by the thousand at weekends, playing techno with a leavening of house. There's even a Besódromo (Kissadrome), where a bevy of lovelies will squeeze you. Forget taxi lines: take the special train.

☎ 96 178 17 06 ✉ Carretera Valencia-Alicante, El Romani ⏰ from midnight Fri & Sat, from 6pm Sun 🚆 departs Estación del Norte at 1.15am, departs El Romani at 6.15am Ⓟ

Dub Club (3, B3)

This bar's a recent and most welcome newcomer to the Valencian club scene. 'We play music not noise' is the slogan, and it indeed offers great music and great variety with reggae (Thursday), dub, drum 'n' bass, funk and more. Tuesday is live-jazz jamming night.

🖥 www.dubclubvalencia.com in Spanish ✉ Calle Jesús 91 € free-€10 ⏰ Thu-Sun 🚌 9, 10, 11, 17, 71 ♿ fair

Flamingo (4, A1)

If you've made it through the night and still have energy to spare, move on to Malvarrosa and Flamingo's Misa de Ocho (Eight O'Clock Mass). Here, you can dance on to house and techno from 8am until 3pm every Sunday morning and sometimes on Saturdays too.

☎ 96 355 64 63 ✉ Isabel de Villena 57 Ⓜ Eugenia Viñes ♿ good

La Claca (2, D4)

With a couple of rooms, La Claca has nightly DJs playing funk, hip hop and indie. On Wednesday, there's theatre. Earmark 11.30pm Sunday for some of the best live flamenco in town. It also gives flamenco classes if you fancy expanding your dance-floor repertoire.

☎ 669 325079 🖥 www.laclaca.com in Spanish ✉ Calle San Vicente Màrtir 3 ⏰ 7pm-3.30am 🚌 4, 8, 9, 31, 70

La Marxa (2, C3)

Subtle it ain't but raucous, thumping, pumping La Marxa is a long-standing Valencian institution and popular late-late choice, if you're still eager for more action. It pulls in all sorts from hardened local party-goers to international students fresh in town

SLEEP DEPRIVATION

This statistic will come as no surprise to you if you've stayed up into the small hours, mingling with the crowds and traffic almost as dense as at rush hour: the average *valenciano*, research reveals, sleeps for only six hours out of every 24. You may well find yourself surviving on even less…

OJOS DE BRUJO

Even though this flamenco fusion band (www.ojosdebrujo.com in Spanish) was recently garlanded by the BBC as Best European Group, they risk giving hardline purists a heart attack. Flamenco rhythms are their starting point, onto which they graft hip hop, reggae, rumba and even Indian tabla. First coming together as a band in Valencia, they spend much of their time touring these days and have recently spent time wowing fans in Mexico, the USA and Canada.

and out for something a little raw.

☎ 96 391 70 65 ⊠ Calle Cocinas 5 € free ⏰ 11pm-3am Thu-Sat 🚌 5B

Latex Club (3, B1)

From the Barrio del Carmen, it's a short walk over Puente San José and up Avenida Constitución to this heaving club north of the river bed. There's a pair of pistes: Latex, experimental and electro; and Freestyle Floor, where anything and everything goes.

☎ 651 883868 ⊠ Calle Doctor Montoro € €12 ⏰ 2-7.30am Fri & Sat 🚌 6, 16, 26, 36

Le Club (3, D4)

Behind the big Pabellón Fuente San Luis sportsdrome, this discoteca has three zones: one for house, another for drum 'n' bass and a retro one, specialising in 1960s and '70s sounds. Mix in more than a little techno and you've something to appeal to every raver.

☎ 96 332 23 27 🖥 www .produccionesuhf.com in Spanish ⊠ Carretera Fuente en Corts 36 € €10-12 ⏰ 1-7.30am Fri & Sat 🚌 13, 14

Radio City (2, B4)

Almost as much mini–cultural centre as club, Radio City,

always seething, knows how to pull in the punters with everything from flamenco (11pm Tuesday), seasonal theatre, cinema and dance – and free disco dancing on Friday and Saturday nights.

☎ 96 391 41 51 🖥 www .radiocityvalencia.com in Spanish ⊠ Calle Santa Teresa 19 ⏰ 7.30pm-3.30am 🚌 7, 60, 81 ♿ fair

CINEMAS

Disgracefully for a city the size of Valencia, which becomes

more cosmopolitan daily, few commercial cinema offers undubbed films (compare what's on offer in Madrid or Barcelona and weep). To its credit, there is a great public-sector option with a weekly cheap day, and there are some excellent multiscreen art-house alternatives.

Albatros (3, E1)

Multiscreen Albatros shows exclusively undubbed films (billed in the listings as VO, meaning *version originale*).

Is it a bird? Nope, Albatros is one of the main cinemas

When in Valencia, cinephiles also seek out Babel

You can take in excellent indie, Sundance-style and mainstream films in English and other languages, though it rarely shows blockbusters. There's a café attached and you can buy a combined cinema and snack ticket.

☎ 96 393 26 77 ☐ www .cinesalbatrosbabel.com in Spanish ✉ Plaza Fray Luis Colomer 4 € tickets €5.20, Mon €4.20 ⏲ at 5.30pm, 8pm & 11pm, also at 1am Fri & Sat 🚌 10, 18, 79, 80, 90 ♿ good

Babel (3, D2)
Sister to the Albatros, Babel offers the same adventurous programming for cinephiles.

☎ 96 362 67 95 ☐ www .cinesalbatrosbabel.com in Spanish ✉ Calle Vicente Sancho Tello 10 € tickets €5.20, Mon €4.20 ⏲ at 5.30pm, 8pm & 11pm, also at 1am Fri & Sat 🚌 18, 29, 30, 31 ♿ good

Filmoteca (2, D5)
On the 4th floor of the Teatro Rialto building, the excellent Filmoteca screens undubbed

classic, art-house and experimental films. Programming can range from a François Truffaut retrospective to the greatest epics of Molvanian cinema. In August it goes open-air, screening late-night films in the Jardines del Turia, below the Palau de la Música.

☎ 96 399 55 77 ☐ www .ivac-lafilmoteca.es in Spanish ✉ Plaza del Ayuntamiento € tickets €1.50 ⏲ at 6pm, 8pm & 10.30pm Tue-Sun Ⓜ Xàtiva 🚌 4, 6, 10, 36 ♿ good

CLASSICAL MUSIC, OPERA & THEATRE

Palau de la Música (3, D3)
This huge, glass-domed concert hall, above the Jardines del Turia, hosts mainly classical-music recitals. Each year, it attracts the very best of touring orchestras, which play in its acoustically impressive Sala Iturbi. The more intimate Sala Rodriguez is used for ensemble and chamber recitals.

☎ 96 337 50 20 ☐ www .palaudevalencia.com in Spanish ✉ Paseo de la Alameda 30 Ⓜ Alameda ♿ fair

Palau de les Arts Reina Sofía (3, D4)
This monumental structure with its four auditoriums (see also p25) had its gala opening in October 2005 then, as is the wont with such public buildings, closed down again so that it could be completed. Regular programming was expected to begin in autumn 2006.

☎ 902 100031 ☐ www .cac.es ✉ Autovía a El Saler 🚌 13, 15, 35, 40, 95 Ⓟ ♿ fair

Teatro Principal (2, D5)
The Teatro Principal, underwritten by the provincial government, is Valencia's main venue for opera, theatre and dance. It brings in both national and international touring companies. Over 150 years old, its interior is an architectural jewel.

☎ 96 353 92 00 ✉ Calle Barcas 15 Ⓜ Xàtiva 🚌 5, 6, 13, 62, 81 ♿ fair

Teatro Olympia (2, C5)
Teatro Olympia, privately owned, offers a varied and intermittent diet of visiting shows, national and occasionally international. Unlike the public-sector competition, it has to pay its way so often falls back on comedy, safe potboilers or dance.
☎ 96 351 73 15 ✉ Calle San Vicente Mártir 🚌 7, 27, 71, 72, 81 ♿ fair

Teatro Rialto (2, D5)
In the same building as the Filmoteca, Teatro Rialto also belongs to the regional government. It promotes mainly local drama and dance. Many of the plays it puts on are in *valenciano*.
☎ 96 353 93 00 ✉ Plaza del Ayuntamiento 17 Ⓜ Xàtiva 🚌 4, 6, 10, 36 ♿ good

NOISE
Spain, it's attested, is the world's noisiest country after Japan – and in Valencia the decibel counter runs at its highest. Mainly it's the traffic din on busy highways but residents complain bitterly about the human racket, especially at bar throwing-out time.

Around the Barrio del Carmen, you'll see banners draped from balconies with slogans such as *Respetad el descanso de los vecinos* ('Respect neighbours' right to rest'), *'Soroll no! Volem dormir'* ('No to noise! We want to sleep') and *'Estem farts'* (not what you might think but 'We've had enough').

GAY & LESBIAN VALENCIA

There's a small gay rect-angle at the west end of the Barrio del Carmen, where most of the enticing venues beckon.

Café de la Seu (2, C3)
Cathedral Café, up a side street and only a few metres from the eponymous cathedral, is a relaxing, gay-friendly place to enjoy a jug of Agua de Valencia, one of the creative cocktails, or something soft from its wide range of infusions.
☎ 96 391 57 15 ✉ Calle Santo Cáliz 7 🕒 6pm-1.30am Mon-Thu, 6pm-2am Fri & Sat 🚌 4, 6, 8, 70, 71

Café Sant Miguel (2, B3)
With soft background music and a summer terrace, this is the place to meet, converse, see and be seen. Inside, it's all gleaming white, mini-malist and seductive. The food's more colourful but equally entrancing.
☎ 96 392 31 29 ✉ Plaza Sant Miguel 13 🕒 7.30-11.30pm Tue-Sun winter, daily summer 🚌 5B, 7, 81 ♿ good

Deseo 54 (3, C1)
Definitely for the younger stay-through-till-dawn crowd, the music here, mainly pop remixes, makes for awesome dancing. If you stay late enough (and the action continues until way past dawn), you'll enjoy a great drag show.
🖥 www.deseo54.com in Spanish ✉ Calle Pepita 15 € €10 🕒 from 1.30am Sat

Sauna Magnus Termas
(3, D2)
Of Valencia's several exclusively gay saunas, Magnus Termas is indeed on the grand scale. There's a pool, hot tub, equally hot videos, bar, steam room and plenty of private cabins for private pleasures. Thursday, when admission is reduced to €10.50, is particularly busy. ☎ 96 337 48 92 ✉ Avenida del Puerto 27 € 13 🕙 10am-midnight 🚌 1, 2, 3, 4, 30 ♿ fair

Venial (2, B3)
With its house and techno music, Venial is far and away the city's most popular gay dance venue, and it's particularly popular with the younger crowd. If you prefer something more relaxed, there's a quieter chill-out zone. It's also big on cabarets and theme nights. ☎ 96 391 73 56 🖳 www.venialvalencia.com in Spanish ✉ Calle Quart 26 🕙 1-7.30am 🚌 5B, 7, 81

SPORT

FOOTBALL
Both Valencia's professional football teams normally play home games on Sundays between September and May.

Valencia Club de Fútbol
(3, D2)
Valencia, the European Cup runners-up in 2000 and 2001, Spanish League Champions 2003 and 2004, and UEFA cup holders in 2004, play at the Estadio Luis Casanova. Call for a **tour** (☎ 96 360 17 10;

€1; 🕙 9am-2pm & 3-7pm Mon-Fri) of the stadium Match tickets (€18-60) are sold at the stadium and club shop. ☎ 96 337 26 26 🖳 www.valenciacf.es ✉ Avenida Aragón 🕙 10am-9pm Mon-Sat Ⓜ Aragón ♿ fair

Valencia Club de Fútbol Shop (3, D2)
The seriously soccer-crazy might want to pick up a scarf, flag, woolly hat or shirt from the official club shop, where you can also buy tickets for forthcoming matches. ☎ 96 351 47 42 ✉ Calle Pintor Sorolla 25 🕙 10am-9pm Mon-Sat 🚌 6, 28, 32, 70, 71 ♿ fair

Levante UD
In 2004–05, after more than 20 years' absence, Levante won promotion to the Spanish first division – and promptly dropped back down again. In need of your support, they play on the north side of town. You should have no trouble picking up a ticket (€12-36) at the ground

on match day. ☎ 902 22 03 04 🖳 www.levanteud.com in Spanish ✉ Avenida Hermanos Machado s/n Ⓜ Machado Ⓟ ♿ fair ♿

BASKETBALL
Pamesa (3, D4)
Professional basketball team Pamesa regularly finish in the top half of the Spanish professional league. They play at the Pabellón Fuente San Luis. Buy tickets (€15-80) online or at the club shop in the sportsdrome. ☎ 96 395 70 84 🖳 www.pamesabasket.com in Spanish ✉ Avenida Hermanos Maristas s/n 🚌 13, 14 Ⓟ ♿ fair

BULLFIGHTING
Bullfights, should they figure in your lexicon as a sport, usually coincide with local fiestas, such as Las Fallas and the Feria de Julio. They take place in the **Plaza de Toros** (2, D6; ☎ 96 351 93 15; Calle Xàtiva s/n), which can accommodate over 20,000 spectators.

Estadio Luis Casanova, where Valencia footballers play

Sleeping

It seems that several new mid-range hotels pop up in Valencia each year, catering primarily to savvy business travellers during the week, families at weekends and travellers every day of the year.

Prices vary hugely (in one instance by 300%), especially in midrange and top-end hotels that cater to business travellers. The high-season rates we quote cumulatively only apply for about 30 days each year. They're slapped on for major national holidays such as Semana Santa (Easter Week), local festivities such as Las Fallas and major trade fairs, such as the Feria del Mueble (Furniture Fair) in September. Lowest rates usually kick in at weekends (Friday and Saturday nights, sometimes Sunday too) and throughout the month of August (July also in some cases).

Most hotels in Valencia display the full range of tariffs on their

New boutique hotel Palau de la Mar (p70)

websites or will respond to an email query. If not, the city's tourist offices can advise travellers on accommodation options.

There's no shortage of balconies to serenade your loved one at Ad Hoc (p71)

TOP END

Hotel Astoria Palace
(2, D5)
Although facing increasingly keen competition from much younger luxury upstarts around the Ciudad de las Artes y las Ciencias, Hotel Astoria remains a popular choice among visiting dignitaries and theatre folk playing Teatro Principal. Almost 50 years in business, it can still hold its own for top-end comfort and attentive service.
☎ 96 398 10 00 🖳 www .hotel-astoria-palace.com ✉ Plaza Rodrigo Botet 5 🚌 4, 6, 10, 19, 36 Ⓜ Xàtiva ♿ good 🍴 on-site restaurant, Vinatea

Las Arenas
(4, A2)
Opened in early 2006, huge beachside hotel Las Arenas, built in an arc around an old spa, is the newest of Valencia's five-star hotels. Higher rooms have sensational views of the coastline and port. There's an ultramodern new spa and two pools (one heated and open year-round).
☎ 96 312 06 00 🖳 www .hotel-lasarenas.com ✉ Calle Eugenia Viñes 22-24 🚌 1, 2, 32 🚋 Les Arenas 🏊 ♿ good 🍴 on-site restaurant

Neptuno
(4, B3)
The Neptuno, the only quality medium-sized hotel overlooking the beach, is a very stylish, ultramodern, upmarket newcomer. Popular with business visitors, it's also an ideal choice if you want to mix cultural tourism in the heart of town with a little beach frolicking.
☎ 96 356 77 77 🖳 www .hotelneptunovalencia.com ✉ Paseo de Neptuno 2 🚌 1, 2, 19, 32 🚋 Les Arenas ♿ fair 🍴 superb on-site gourmet restaurant, Tridente

Palau de la Mar
(2, F5)
Created recently by the merging of two elegant 19th-century mansions (with 18 very similar rooms, newly constructed, surrounding a tranquil internal garden), this boutique hotel, all black, white, soft fuscous and beige, is cool, confident and ultramodern. There's a sauna, Jacuzzi – and a pool scarcely bigger than your bathtub.
☎ 96 316 28 84 🖳 www .hospes.es ✉ Calle Navarro Reverter 14 🚌 2, 4, 10, 71 Ⓜ Alameda 🏊 ♿ good 🍴 magnificent on-site restaurant, Ampar

Puerta Valencia
(3, E2)
An ultramodern, arty option, Puerta Valencia's corridors and rooms are hung with original abstract-art canvases. Step beyond the dreary surroundings into this huge glass cube and cocoon yourself within. Staff are young, keen and friendly, rooms large and tastefully furnished.
☎ 96 393 63 95 🖳 www .hoteles-silken.com ✉ Avenida Cardenal Benlloch 28 🚌 18, 89, 90 Ⓜ Aragón ♿ good 🍴 excellent on-site restaurant

MIDRANGE

Abba Acteón
(3, E3)
Though not as new as some of the parvenus around the Ciudad de las Artes y las Ciencias, the Acteón is pleasantly avant-garde, well priced and extremely well maintained. Its large bedrooms make maximum use of space.
☎ 96 331 07 07 🖳 www .abba-acteonhotel.com ✉ Calle Vicente Beltrán Grimal 2 🚌 1, 2, 3, 4, 30 ♿ good 🍴 on-site bar & restaurant

Indulge in comfort at the Hotel Astoria Palace

Petit Palace Bristol (p72)

AC Valencia (3, E3)
Three kilometres from the heart of town and an easy walk from the Ciudad de las Artes y las Ciencias, this hotel, established in 2003 and typical of the AC group, has an ultra-contemporary feel and offers exceptional value low-season rates (which include most weekends).
☎ 96 331 70 00 ⌨ www
.ac-hotels.com ✉ Avenida de Francia 67 🚍 19
🅿 per night €8 ♿ good
✗ on-site restaurant 🛉

Ad Hoc (2, E3)
Friendly, welcoming Ad Hoc offers comfort and charm deep within the old quarter and also runs a splendid restaurant with only 10 tiny tables. The late-19th-century building has been restored to its former splendour with great sensitivity, revealing original ceilings, mellow brickwork and solid wooden beams.
☎ 96 391 91 40
⌨ www.adhochoteles.com

✉ Calle Boix 4 🚍 2, 5, 16, 28, 80 ♿ fair ✗ on-site restaurant

Atarazanas (3, F3)
Only a busy highway separates this squat, cuboid block from the old port. But the soundproofing is excellent and comfortable, while well-furnished rooms overlook a couple of quiet squares. For the best views, choose one of the six double-window corner rooms (whose room numbers coincidentally all end in 06).
☎ 96 320 30 10 ⌨ www
.sh-hoteles.com ✉ Plaza Tribunal de las Aguas 5
🚍 1, 2, 3, 19, 30 ♿ fair
✗ on-site bar & restaurant

Cónsul del Mar (3, D3)
In an earlier incarnation the residence of the Portuguese consul to Valencia, this hotel became affiliated to the Barceló group in late 2005, coincidentally its centennial year. It sparkles within from the thorough makeover it received, while retaining the best of the original structure. There's a small heated pool.
☎ 96 362 54 32 ⌨ www
.barcelo.com ✉ Avenida del Puerto 39 🚍 1, 2, 4, 30, 40 🅿 per day €11
🛥 ♿ fair ✗ Take a bus to La Pepica (p58)

Express Las Artes (3, E4)
Shorn-down sister to the more luxurious NH hotel Las Artes next door, it's a short stroll from the Ciudad de las Artes y las Ciencias (and offers attractive accommodation-with-admission packages). A cosy option despite its breathless title, it's ideal for a brief stopover and has especially tempting weekend rates.
☎ 96 335 60 62 ⌨ www
.nh-hoteles.com ✉ Avenida Instituto Obrero de Valencia 26 🚍 15, 35, 95 🅿 limited, per night €12.25 ✗ restaurant at Las Artes 🛉

Inglés (2, D4)
The Inglés occupies an elegant, much modified 18th-century palace. One side overlooks a pedestrian square and the National Ceramics Museum; another the city's swankiest shopping street. Service is friendly and attentive, and the café has a pleasant terrace overlooking the museum's exuberant façade.
☎ 96 351 64 26 ⌨ www
.meliaingles.solmelia.com
✉ Calle Marqués de Los Dos Aguas 6 🚍 4, 6, 8, 26, 31
♿ good ✗ on-site café & restaurant

WEEKEND & SUMMER BARGAINS

Valencia, with its busy annual programme of fairs and conventions, attracts business visitors by the tens of thousands. One happy consequence for short-breakers is that many midrange and top-end hotels offer enticingly lower rates at weekends, when commercial visitors have flown their temporary nests.

Most such places also drop their rates substantially in August, when most of Spain is on the beaches or in the mountains.

Jardín Botánico has flair

Jardín Botánico (3, B2)
Welcoming and megacool ('Chill Out' is its slogan), this intimate – only 16 rooms – hotel is furnished with great flair. Well priced within its category, it adds grace to an unfashionable part of town. Understandably, the Instituto Valenciano de Arte Moderno (IVAM), an easy walk away, regularly selects it as a venue for its guests.

☎ 96 315 40 12 🖳 www .hoteljardinbotanico.com ✉ Calle Doctor Peset Cervera 6 🚌 2, 60, 61, 62, 63 Ⓜ Turia ✕ Les Níts (p51)

Las Artes (3, E4)
This hotel sits well among the ultramodern buildings that pull the city's centre of gravity eastwards. Appealing particularly to business travellers, it also courts young families. Like the simpler Express Las Artes next door, it does accommodation-with-admission packages to the Ciudad de las Artes y las Ciencias. There's a sauna, gym and heated pool.

☎ 96 335 13 10 🖳 www .nh-hoteles.com ✉ Avenida Instituto Obrero de Valencia 28 🚌 15, 35, 95 Ⓟ limited: per night €12.25 🛴 ♿ good ✕ on-site restaurant ♠ free for under 12s sharing with parents

Petit Palace Bristol (2, D4)
Stylish, minimalist and friendly, this lovely boutique hotel, a comprehensively made-over 19th-century noble mansion, retains the best of its past. It's well worthwhile paying €10 extra for one of the superior doubles on the top (5th) floor. You'll enjoy a particularly scrumptious buffet breakfast.

☎ 96 394 51 00 🖳 www .hthoteles.com ✉ Calle Abadía San Martín 3 🚌 4, 6, 8, 19, 36 Ⓜ Xàtiva ♿ good ✕ Sagardí (p52)

Petit Palace Germanías (3, C3)
Younger sibling of Petit Palace Bristol and inaugurated in 2004, this equally boutique hotel is on the west, unfashionable side of the Gran Vía. But its bright façade beckons and, once within, you'll find its tasteful, minimally furnished rooms just as seductive.

☎ 96 351 36 38 🖳 www .hthotels.com ✉ Calle Sueca 14 🚌 1, 2, 41, 79, 80 Ⓜ Xàtiva Ⓟ per night €12 ♿ good ✕ El México de María (p55)

Sorolla (2, C6)
This comfortable hotel, wedged at the intersection of two pedestrian streets, is well positioned for public transport. The streets below buzz with life on warm evenings but you'll sleep well; double-glazed windows effectively parry the street-level hubbub. Top- (8th-) floor rooms (€15 extra) each have a broad terrace with bird's-eye views.

☎ 96 352 33 92 🖳 www .hotelsorolla.com ✉ Calle Convento Santa Clara 5 🚌 4, 6, 10, 19, 36 Ⓜ Xàtiva ♿ fair ✕ Commo (p50)

Venecia (2, C5)
Excellent value except during its brief high season, the

DOUBLE ROOM & DOUBLE BED
Non-Spanish visitors sometimes complain that the hotel booking they made has not been honoured to the letter. But often it's simply a question of linguistic confusion rather than inefficiency. If you book a double room *(habitación doble)*, you'll probably be allocated one with twin beds, something that can present a challenge to those on an amorous outing. If you want to snuggle together, be sure to specify a double bed *(cama matrimonial)* when you reserve.

Venecia's other strong points are exceptionally friendly service and its prime location. Rooms overlook either busy Plaza del Ayuntamiento or pedestrianised Calle en Llop, onto which the hotel entrance gives.

☎ 96 352 42 67 💻 www .hotelvenecia.com ✉ Calle en Llop 5 🚍 4, 6, 10, 19, 36 Ⓜ Xàtiva ♿ fair 🍽 Cardamom (p50)

BUDGET

Hôme Deluxe Hostel
(2, C3)
This original, welcoming, traveller-savvy haven has self-catering facilities, wi-fi and oodles of useful lowdown about Valencia. All 10 rooms are individually designed. How about Sexy Love with its ceiling mirror? Luce, all in white? The Safari room? Reservations are normally essential.

☎ 96 391 46 91 💻 www.likeathome.net

OTHER RECOMMENDED HOSTELS
Albergue Ciudad de Valencia (2, B4; ☎ 96 392 51 00; www.alberguedevalencia.com; Calle Balmes 17) Valencia's Hostelling International (HI) hostel.
Hôme Backpackers (2, B3; ☎ 96 391 37 97; www .likeathome.net; Plaza Vicente Iborra s/n)
Hôme Youth Hostel (2, C4; ☎ 96 391 62 29; www .likeathome.net; Calle Lonja 4)
Indigo Youth Hostel (2, A4; ☎ 96 315 39 88; www .indigohostel.com; Calle Guillem de Castro 64)

✉ Calle Cadirers 11 🚍 7, 27, 28, 81 ♿ fair 🍽 La Pappardella (p51)

Hostal Antigua Morellana (2, C4)
This friendly, family-run place, originally an 18th-century inn, offers exceptional value. It's intimate (only 18 rooms) and immaculately kept. All rooms have air-con and those overlooking the quiet street have little balconies. Bathrooms, equipped with shower but no bathtub, are squeaky clean.

☎ 96 391 57 73 💻 www .hostalam.com ✉ Calle

En Bou 2 🚍 7, 27, 28, 81 ♿ fair 🍽 Tasca Ángel (p53)

Nest Youth Hostel (2, E4)
As cosy as its name implies, the Nest is a cheerful hostel, run by seasoned travellers. It sits cheekily amid the swanky apartments and shops of this fashionable street. Brightly decorated rooms range from doubles to dorms accommodating 12. There's a well-equipped kitchen and, up top under the eaves, a large lounge.

☎ 96 342 71 68 💻 www .nestyh.com ✉ Calle Paz 36 🚍 6, 8, 11, 71 Ⓜ Colón 🍽 La Utielana (p51)

Pensión París (2, D5)
Rooms are spotless, and communal bathrooms scrubbed and gleaming at this enticing option, the antithesis of the crowded, pack-'em-in hostel. All 15 rooms overlook the quiet street. Nos 105 and 306 have large, glassed-in balconies. Mattresses are firm and triple rooms especially large.

☎ 96 352 67 66 💻 .pensionparis.com ✉ Salvá 12 🚍 6, 8, 32 Ⓜ Colón ♿ 🍽 Neco (p52)

Rooms are certainly individual at Hôme Deluxe Hostel

HISTORY

Valencia's first known permanent settlement began in 138 BC, when Roman legionnaires were granted prime river-side land to build themselves a retirement community, which they named 'Valentia'. As Roman Imperial power waned, the town was scarcely touched by the Visigoth invasions from north of the Pyrenees, which had a major impact upon the rest of the Mediterranean peninsula.

The influence of Muslims was much more fundamental and long-standing. Arabs established the still-extant ceramics industry of Manises and Paterna, west of Valencia, improved irrigation techniques and introduced the water

Another legendary knight in Valencia – El Cid

wheel, rice (still grown all around the Albufera freshwater lagoon) and oranges, the region's most important contemporary cash crop.

The legendary Castilian knight El Cid briefly interrupted Muslim rule in 1094 but Jaime I definitively retook the city only in 1238. His most important legacy to Valencia was its Fueros, a charter guaranteeing the region considerable independence from the crown of Aragón.

Gold Turns To Dust

Valencia enjoyed its *siglo de oro* (golden age) in the 15th century, 200 years before the rest of Spain, when it was one of the Mediterranean's strongest trading centres. Then, the magnificent Lonja, Palau de la

...eneralitat (p26) is one of many beautiful 15th-century buildings

Generalitat and Torres de Quart were constructed. However, in 1492, the very year in which the Moors lost Granada, their last foothold in Spain, all Jews were expelled from Spain, leaving Valencia bereft of many of its most important financiers and skilled artisans. The impact of this forced relocation, however, was as nothing compared to the early-17th-century expulsion of the Moriscos – Arabs who had remained in the region after the Reconquista. In just five years an estimated 170,000 souls left by sea. Much of the interior was severely underpopulated and a whole social layer of craftsmen and water managers was skimmed off. The middle classes, too, were affected – to such an extent that in 1613 the Banco Municipal de Valencia went bankrupt. Reeling from such blows, the Valencia region, which for two centuries had outshone Catalonia, lost a superiority that it was never again to recover.

Like Catalonia, Valencia backed the wrong horse in the War of the Spanish Succession (1702–13) and in retribution the victorious Bourbon king, Felipe V, abolished Valencia's Fueros. A century later, in 1812, Valencia again suffered when French forces under Marshal Suchet besieged and occupied the city.

Industry & Wars

In the 19th century the silk industry employed more than 25,000 workers until it was decimated by a combination of disease and competition from Lyon in France. Wool from the interior was also exported through the city. Of even greater significance for the landscape today, citrus farming rapidly expanded and tonne upon tonne of oranges destined for France, UK and Germany were exported through Valencia's port.

Although Spain did not participate in WWI, the Comunidad Valenciana was hit hard economically. When Germany began to blockade boats bearing oranges to enemy countries, whole orchards were ripped out. Sales of wine from the Comunidad slumped too. Only the trade in rice, imported by all sides as a food staple, remained buoyant.

When, on 17 July 1936, General Francisco Franco led the army in his nationalist uprising that sparked the Spanish Civil War, Valencia unanimously opted for the republican cause. As the

Whoa! King Jaime I, Plaza de la Glorieta

nationalist noose around Madrid was tugged tighter in November, the republican government – the legally elected government – moved to the city, decamping to Barcelona just under a year later. From 1937 it was subjected to enemy bombardment. In 1939 Valencia and Alicante were the last loyal cities to be overcome by nationalist forces.

Hard Times

General Franco kept Spain out of WWII and the country suffered a UN-sponsored trade boycott. The years that followed are known as the *años de hambre* (years of hunger). Only in the late 1950s did Valencia return to pre–Civil War economic levels. Progress was steady and swift. The ceramic, textile and shoemaking sections began to thrive, but the greatest impact came from tourism. Even so, thousands of *valencianos* crossed the Pyrenees, seeking work in prosperous countries such as France, Germany and Switzerland. Internally, a shorter migration route led from the interior to Valencia city and coastal resorts, leaving much of the interior underpopulated.

With the death of Franco in 1975, regionalism once more became respectable. The Fueros may not have been restored but, benefiting from the decentralisation that followed Franco's death, Valencia and its region today enjoy a high degree of autonomy. The Valencian language too, thanks to a regional TV station and compulsory courses in schools, has become, for many, a source of regional pride.

Graffiti. A global environmental concern?

ENVIRONMENT

Water is an increasing preoccupation: 2005 was the Valencian region's driest year since the 1930s. Water rationing was introduced during the summer months in 2001. Every summer the dams of the hinterland that supply the town fail to fully replenish. But it's a problem shared with much of Spain and a controversial plan to divert waters from the River Ebro, claimed by both Aragón and Catalonia, has been shelved. All the same, the streets of the city are sluiced down nightly with thousands of litres of water, mostly recycled, that gurgles away down drains.

Rubbish, too, is collected on a nightly basis. There are street containers for glass, paper and plastic but many inhabitants just dump everything in the nearest all-purpose skip.

Valencia has an excellent integrated public transport system. Most buses have disabled access, and an increasing number run on natural

Take a fast tram to the coastal promenade

gas or recycled cooking oil. Even so, it's difficult to prise car owners from their beloved vehicles: main arteries get clogged and parking can induce apoplexy.

GOVERNMENT & POLITICS

Confusing stuff but Valencia city is the principal town and capital of Valencia province, which in its turn fits within the Comunidad Valenciana (the Valencia region) – of which Valencia city is also the capital. These days, the Comunidad Valenciana, one of 17 semi-autonomous regions of Spain, enjoys a degree of control over its affairs that it hasn't had since 1707, when its Fueros (p75) was abrogated. The Ayuntamiento (Town Hall) has the greatest impact upon citizens' everyday lives. Both, as a result of local elections in 2003, are in the hands of the right-wing Partido Popular (People's Party; PP). Since the national government in Madrid is controlled by the Partido Socialista Obrero Espanol (Spanish Socialist Worker Party, PSOE), there's constant bickering, accusation and counter-accusation between central and Valencian regional organs.

ECONOMY

Sunshine – over 300 days a year of it – is one of the city's most valuable, yet completely free, commodities. Very few visitors come to town primarily to soak up the sun but tens of thousands of holidaymakers from the coastal resorts of the Costa Blanca come up for the day. It's been said that the sun's rays entice more than four million visitors annually. The sun also kisses the crops and fruit trees of the coastal

And they say there are more than 300 cloudless days in Valencia each year ...

plain and interior hills, produce which finds its way to Valencia's markets and supermarkets or is shipped abroad through the port or by truck. Annual tonnage may be declining but rice, primarily from the paddy fields around the Albufera lake, is another staple export.

Industrially, with one exception there's no major player and all to the good. Small-scale operations prevail, except for the Ford motor company, which was threatening to downsize and take business elsewhere, where production costs are cheaper, at the time of writing.

SOCIETY & CULTURE

The people of the Levante, as this stretch of Mediterranean coast is commonly called, have the reputation of being joyous, convivial and noisy, traits that find their expression in Las Fallas, the quintessential *valenciano* festival. The people are great eaters-out, who like to stay up late. Like most Spaniards, they prefer their pleasures away from home, as you'll quickly discover if you're out and about any night between Wednesday and Saturday. Many have a second home, either a villa or the traditional family house, within reasonable driving distance, to which they take off on summer weekends.

> **DID YOU KNOW?**
> - Valencia's population is 791,000
> - Between 2001 and 2004, the number of visitors to Valencia rose by 27%
> - In the first six months of 2005, non-Spanish visitors increased by over 20%, compared to the equivalent half of 2004
> - In the two days of La Ofrenda, during Las Fallas, more than half a million carnations are offered to the Virgin Mary

When is an orange a Valencian?

> **DOS & DON'TS**
> As in many countries, *valencianos* tend not to spray 'please' and 'thank you' around as liberally as many Anglo-Saxons. This is simply linguistic custom and doesn't imply any lack of appreciation. By contrast, many will instinctively mutter a *buenos días* (good day) or *adios* (goodbye) when entering or leaving a café or shop and would be perplexed by the way many northern Europeans slink in and out. Again, it's just social convention.
>
> Men and women, women and women greet each other, even if it's for the first time, with a light kiss on each cheek; peck right then left.
>
> You'll have a tough time if you're sensitive to tobacco smoke. Smoking is more and more controlled in public places such as cinemas and government offices, though smokeless bars and restaurants, or even a zone within them, scarcely exist (this may change once new legislation, rolling through its procedural stages, kicks in).
>
> Quite a lot of *valencianos* hold firm opinions on the role of the Valencian language and the region's relations with Catalonia and central government. Unless you know well those you're talking with, you're probably better off just nodding sympathetically.

ARTS
Architecture

The three distinct portals of Valencia's cathedral (p8) give a rapid overview of how the Romanesque, Gothic and baroque each manifested itself in local ecclesiastical architecture. Mediterranean Gothic's most exuberant flourishing, by contrast, was in the temporal rather than spiritual domain.

There's more to La Lonja's entrance door...

Coinciding with Valencia's 15th-century golden age, it informs monumental public buildings such as La Lonja (p13) and the Palau de la Generalitat (p26).

The Renaissance reached Valencia from Italy earlier than elsewhere in Spain (the infamous Borgia family, ensconced in Rome, came from Gandía, just down the coast), but it was of relatively minor architectural importance. The baroque had an altogether more profound impact. Few churches were constructed from scratch in baroque style. However, coinciding with another time of economic prosperity for the city, many were embellished with elaborate *retablos* – huge gilded, painted altarpieces that dwarf the altar itself. From this period too comes the magnificent octagonal bell tower of Iglesia de Santa Catalina (p25), soaring skywards above the original Gothic place of worship.

The restatement of classical architectural principles that informs much 19th-century Spanish architecture is evident in many of the bourgeois domestic buildings of the Eixample. By far the most significant public building from this time is the Plaza de Toros (bullring; p68), which is a vast, strictly symmetrical and deeply pleasing colonnaded structure. Altogether more original was Modernismo (similar to Art Nouveau), an artistic movement that originated in Catalonia and whose most famous proponent is Antoni Gaudí. See p33 for a 45-minute walking tour that highlights Valencia's best, including the splendid Estación del Norte, Mercado Central and Mercado de Colón.

Contemporary Valencian architect Santiago Calatrava (p26) picks up the traditions of Modernismo with its favouring of *trencadí* (tile-shard mosaic) and shapes deriving from nature. Creating primarily in

Palau de les Arts Reína Sofia: a tribute to Sydney?

supple, malleable concrete, a material denied to those of an earlier era, he's responsible for most of the architecturally stunning Ciudad de las Artes y las Ciencias (p10).

Painting

Valencia's first painter of lasting renown was Juan de Juanes (c 1500–79), whose sensitive mannerist canvases with their bright patches of colour still decorate many a parish church. From the 17th century, when artists such as Velázquez, Murillo and Zurbarán were active elsewhere in Spain, sprang two local artists who can hold their own with the greatest. Francisco Ribalta (1564–1628) influenced a

View Pinazo's work at Museo de Bellas Artes

generation of artists through his Valencia studio and school. Among his altarpieces with strong interplay of light and shade is his *San Francisco abrazado al crucificado* (San Francisco embracing the crucified Jesus) in Valencia's Museo de Bellas Artes (p11). José de Ribera, renowned for his forceful realism, manages to squeeze in as a scion of Valencia even though in his early twenties he moved to southern Italy, at the time ruled by Spain, where he was known as *il spagnoletto* – the little guy from Spain.

In the second half of the 19th century, artists of what is loosely called the Valencian Impressionist school worked largely to commission, turning out landscapes, portraits that flatter, peasants and fisherfolk, viewed with a somewhat romantic eye. Ignacio Pinazo (1849–1916; see p12), in his portraiture, captured with broad brushstrokes the essence of a subject's character. José Benlliure (1855–1937) records popular traditions and half-recalled customs – a farm worker puffing at a pipe or a peasant with his flask of wine. You can visit his studio (p22).

Joaquín Sorolla (1863–1923), the most famous, also dug deep into the daily life of everyday folk for much of his inspiration. Known as 'the painter of light', he portrays its transient flicker upon water. He too did his share of portraits for hard cash, fixing on canvas prominent personalities from the Valencian society of the day.

There's a vast variety of styles on show in many Valencian galleries

Directory

ARRIVAL & DEPARTURE
Air
Less than five years ago, not one budget airline buzzed in to Valencia. Today eight low-cost flights daily fly to/from UK airports, in addition to national carriers British Airways and Iberia. Other economy flights serve major European destinations such as Milan, Rome, Berlin and Zurich.

Valencia's **Aeropuerto de Manises** (www.aena.es) is 10km west of the centre along the A3, direction Madrid.

INFORMATION
General inquiries & flight information (☎ 96 159 85 00)

AIRPORT ACCESS
The No 5 metro line is currently being extended and will connect the airport, downtown and the port. Projected completion date is early 2007.

Aero-Bus (€2.50, 20 minutes, every 20 minutes, 6am-10pm) leaves from a stop outside the upper, departures area and makes two stops: at metro stations Àngel Guimerà (2, A5) and Bailén (3, C3), the latter just south of Estación del Norte, the main train station.

A taxi into the centre – about a 20-minute ride, depending on traffic density – costs from €12 to €15 (there's a supplement of €2.75 for journeys originating at the airport).

Car parking will remain something of a shambles until late 2006, when extra facilities, under construction to meet the recent surge in passenger numbers, should come on stream. Until then, allow extra time since the temporary overflow park, served by a free shuttle bus, is some distance away.

Train
All trains run by the Spanish state railway **Renfe** (☎ 902 240202; www.renfe. es in Spanish) call at Valencia's **Estación del Norte** (2, C6; metro Xàtiva). There are services almost hourly to both Madrid and Barcelona. *Cercanías* (local trains) run southwards as far as Gandia and follow the coast northwards. The station has a tourist office, car-hire facilities, ATMs and a left-luggage office.

Bus
The **bus station** (3, B1; ☎ 96 346 62 66; Avenida Menéndez Pidal 11; metro Turia) is beside the river bed. Bus 8 connects it to Plaza del Ayuntamiento. **AutoRes** (☎ 902 020999; www.auto-res .net) runs at least eight buses daily to/from Madrid (€21, four hours). **Alsa** (☎ 902 422242; www.alsa.es) serves other Spanish cities, including Barcelona (€22 to €27, 4¼ to five hours). There are two ATMs, a Europcar vehicle-hire booth and left-luggage lockers.

Boat
Acciona Trasmediterránea (☎ 902 454645; www.acciona-trasmediterranea .es) runs car and passenger ferries to Mallorca and Ibiza. Buy your ticket online, at the passenger terminal (4, B4) on Muelle de Poniente, or at any travel agency.

Travel Documents
PASSPORT
There's usually no passport control for visitors arriving from other EU countries. EU citizens, and Swiss and Norwegian nationals, need only a passport or national ID card. If you need a visa, your passport must be valid for several months after your date of entry.

VISA
Nationals of Australia, Canada, Israel, Japan, New Zealand and the USA don't need a visa for tourist visits of up to 90 days. Other nationals and those wishing to stay longer for work or study may require one. Since Spain is a signatory to the Schengen agreement, a visa for Spain is valid for other EU countries that have signed up, and vice versa.

Customs & Duty Free

From an EU country with duty paid, you can bring in a – literally – staggering 110L of beer, 10L of spirits, 90L of wine and 800 cigarettes. But why would you when prices in Spain are almost certainly cheaper than at home? From outside the EU, the allowance is 200 cigarettes or 250g of tobacco, 1L of spirits and 2L of still wine.

Left Luggage

At the train station, the *consigna* (left-luggage) lockers (€3 per 24 hours) are located at the far, south end of platform 6. Those at the bus station (€3.50 per 24 hours) are on the 1st floor.

GETTING AROUND

Valencia has an integrated bus, tram and metro network. EMT buses ply town routes, while MetroBus serves outlying towns and villages. Tourist offices stock maps for both services. However, the action part of Valencia is satisfyingly compact and, except for a sally forth to the coast, you'll probably find yourself walking everywhere.

Travel Passes

Valencia Tourist Card (☎ 900 701818) gives unlimited travel by bus, tram or metro within central Zone A. It costs €6/10/12 per day/two days/three days and also entitles you to discounts at a number of sights, restaurants and shops. Pick one up from the tourist offices at the airport, train station or Plaza de la Reina, participating hotels and some tobacconists *(estancos)*.

A 10-journey Bono Bus costs €5.05 and a T-1 (a one-day travel card) is €3. You can buy both at metro stations, plus most tobacconists and newsagents.

Bus

Most **EMT** (☎ 96 352 83 99; www.emt valencia.es in Spanish) buses run from roughly 6.30am to 10.30pm. After this, night services take over on nine routes until around 1.30am, Sunday to Wednesday, and until 3am, Thursday to Saturday.

Metro

Metrovalencia (☎ 900 461046; www.me trovalencia.com) has an expanding network (see the metro map, inside front cover) with, currently, four lines extending deep into the province. A one-way/return journey within the city belt costs €1.10/1.90 and a Bonometro, valid for 10 rides, is €5.40. Services run between about 6am and 11pm.

Tram

Similarly, the single route of the high-speed tram keeps pushing out to the furthest suburbs. It's the most pleasant way to reach the beach (Eugenia Viñes and Las Arenas tram stops). A single journey costs €1.10 and a carnet of ten tickets is €5.40.

Taxi

Larger companies include **Radio-Taxi** (☎ 96 370 33 33) and **Valencia Taxi** (☎ 96 357 13 13). A green light glowing on the roof, or a *libre* sign behind the windscreen indicates that a vehicle's available. Taxis cost €0.73 per kilometre (€0.84 between 10pm and 6am and at weekends) and waiting time is calculated at €13.10 per hour. The minimum fare is €2.95.

Bicycle

Orange Bikes (2, B4; 96 391 75 51; www .orangebikes.net; Calle Santa Teresa 8) is significantly the most reliable of the few bike-hire options in town. It rents mountain and city bikes (€12.50/25/60 per day/weekend/week) and electric bikes (€15 per day). The engaging young Anglo-Valencian couple who run the shop also do repairs and maintenance and sell bikes, both new and secondhand.

Car & Motorcycle

If you're here on a short visit and Valencia city is your only destination, the best advice is, quite simply, don't drive. Taxis are relatively cheap and plentiful and the public transport system's efficient. However, on the downside, street parking's a huge pain, hotel garage rates can be savage and driving in the Centro Histórico is plain antisocial.

Should you wish to get out of town, the two day-trips that we recommend (p35) are both easily accessible by public transport.

If you're intending to tour around the Comunidad,the following reliable local hire companies operate from Valencia airport:

Javea Cars (☎ 96 579 33 12; www.javea cars.com)

Solmar (☎ 96 646 10 00; www.solmar.es)

Victoria Cars (☎ 96 579 27 61; www.vic toriacars.com)

They're usually substantially less expensive than major multinationals and just as reliable.

Europrars operate from the bus and train stations. At the latter you'll also find Avis and Atesa.

PRACTICALITIES
Business Hours
The following are typical opening hours but do check individual listings:

Banks (8.30am-2pm Mon-Fri; some also open 4-7pm Thu & 9am-1pm Sat)

Central Post Office (8.30am-8.30pm Mon-Fri, 9.30am-2pm Sat)

Offices (9am-2pm & 5-8pm Mon-Fri)

Restaurants (2-4pm & 9pm-midnight) Most close one day per week.

Shops (10am-2pm & 5-8pm Mon-Sat) Many big stores and supermarkets don't close at lunchtime.

Climate & When To Go
Winter skies are generally blue and temperatures bracing but not cold. The summer months of July and August, when the average daily maximum hovers around 30°C and humidity is high, can be rather uncomfortable. Then, simply dunk yourself in the Mediterranean – the *average* temperature is 20°C or higher between June and October.

Rain may fall at any time but is negligible except in spring (March, April and May) and autumn, especially September and October. Even at these times, most days will be sunny rather than overcast. But the downpours, when they come, can be torrential...

Locals abandon the city in droves during August, when many restaurants, bars and shops close. On the positive side, the city's much quieter then and hotel prices are generally at their lowest.

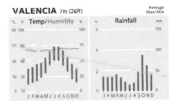

Disabled Travellers
Lots of the newer buses and some metro and tram stations have been adapted for wheelchair access. Street pavements and curbs, by contrast, are often something of a slalom. Major museums and sights all offer reasonable to good disabled access and the situation is improving slowly across the board.

Discounts
Many museums and attractions offer discounts of up to 50% for children under 12 and adults over 65 (be prepared to brandish a passport or other confirmation of your age). Similarly, there are often comparable youth or student rates.

STUDENT & YOUTH CARDS
Most national student organisations can furnish travellers with an **International Student Identity Card** (ISIC; www.isic .org) or **Euro26 card** (for those aged under 26; www.euro26.org).

Electricity
Voltage 220V
Frequency 50Hz
Cycle AC
Plugs Standard continental with two round pins

Embassies & Consulates
All major countries have an embassy in the capital; look them up under Embajadas in Madrid's *Paginas Amarillas* (Yellow Pages).

Of major nations, only the USA maintains a full time **consulate** (2, E5; ☎ 96 351 69 73; 2nd fl, Calle Doctor Romagosa 1; ☺ 10am-2pm Mon-Fri) in Valencia.

Emergencies
Petty theft and pickpocketing are much less of a problem than in Madrid or Barcelona. All the same, keep a weather eye open since tourists are a popular target for the few operators. Car theft is altogether more prevalent, especially if your vehicle has non-Spanish plates. Empty it of everything you value if you park overnight in the street. The same applies if you're driving a hire car.
EU-wide emergency assistance (English-speaking operator; ☎ 112)
Fire (☎ 080)
General emergency (☎ 085)
Policia Nacional (National Police; ☎ 091)
Policia Local (Local Police; ☎ 092)

Fitness
There's no shortage of ways to keep the flab at bay. For absolutely free, you can join the hundreds of joggers who come out at nightfall to trot the 9km length of the Turia river bed. For sea views as you huff and puff, pound the *paseo marítimo* – the broad promenade that extends for over 3km beside the beaches of Las Arenas and La Malvarrosa. Or plough an offshore furrow along the Mediterranean, swimmable for softies between at least June and October and for more hardy souls year-round.

GYMS
Several of the more upmarket hotels have gyms and fitness centres, varying in size from half a floor to what's little more than an extended cupboard. *Polideportivos* are multisports centres that usually have a gym and probably a pool among their facilities. Ask at a tourist office for the hand-out, *Polideportivos Municipales.*

SWIMMING
If sea water up your nostrils makes you sneeze, there are plenty of sweet-water pools, both private and municipal. Tourist offices carry a couple of comprehensive hand-outs, *Piscinas Municipales de Valencia* and *Piscinas No Municipales de Valencia.* Our favourite among the former is the splendid Complexo Deportivo Cultural La Petxina (p24).

Gay & Lesbian Travellers
Gay and lesbian sex are legal in Spain. The age of consent, straight or gay, is 16. Amid considerable controversy and ongoing opposition from conservative and traditional quarters, the central government passed a law, in 2005, making the country Europe's third to accept homosexual marriage and first ever to legalise gay adoption of children.

You could consult the website of the most active local pressure group, www.lambdavalencia.org. However, since it's almost exclusively in *valenciano*, it's opaque to most Spaniards, let alone the rest of the gay universe. For the lowdown on the latest high spots, you're much better off clicking on the Valencia section of www.gaymap.info or, when out and about, picking up a copy of the latest *Shanguide,* a freebie carried by many gay venues.

For our own favourite gay-friendly spots, see pp67-8.

Health
IMMUNISATIONS
There are no specific immunisations required to enter Spain, though should you be

entering from an area where yellow fever is endemic (Africa and South America), you may be asked to flash a certificate of vaccination.

PRECAUTIONS

Valencia's tap water is perfectly safe to drink. The only reason for indulging in bottled mineral water is if the mild back taste of chlorine makes you gag. Transporting what is, after all, simply H_2O long distances is a wasteful use of energy. So, if you prefer the neutral taste of bottled mineral water, choose one of the several options that are drawn from springs within the Valencia region.

Food preparation is, in general, hygienic though bar tapas, even if refrigerated, can look sad and tired by the end of a torrid summer's day.

MEDICAL SERVICES

EU nationals need to carry the new European Health Insurance Card (EHIC) to qualify for free or abated medical treatment in Spain. Consult your local Ministry of Health (eg UK nationals can go www.dh.gov.uk, follow the leads and apply online). Travel insurance is all but essential for other nationalities and recommended as a fall-back for EU citizens too.

For medical treatment go to the reliable public-sector hospitals in Valencia:

Hospital Clínico (3, D1; ☎ 96 386 26 00; Avenida Blasco Ibañez 17)

La Fe (3, A1; ☎ 96 386 27 00; Avenida Campanar 21)

PHARMACIES

All-night pharmacies run on a changing roster. In the window of every pharmacy is a list of the nearest ones currently open through the night.

Feast of San Vicente Mártir 22 January
Feast of San José 19 March
Good Friday March/April
Feast of San Vicente Ferrer Eight days after Easter Sunday
Labour Day 1 May
Corpus Cristi 9th Sunday after Easter
Feast of the Assumption 15 August
Valencian Regional Day 9 October
Spain's National Day 12 October
All Saints Day 1 November
Constitution Day 6 December
Feast of the Immaculate Conception 8 December
Christmas Day 25 December

Internet

There are plenty of Internet and phone centres all over town, many catering to the substantial immigrant population and offering rock-bottom rates. Wi-fi has rapidly become almost de rigueur in midrange and top-end hotels, most of which exact a charge for the privilege.

INTERNET CAFÉS

Ono (2, C5; Calle San Vicente Mártir 22; per hr €3; ☼ 10am-1am)

Work Center (2, D6; ☎ 96 112 08 30; Calle Xàtiva 19; per hr €4; ☼ 24hr)

USEFUL WEBSITES

Ayuntamiento de Valencia (www.valencia.es) Valencia Town Hall.

Barriodelcarmen.net (www.barriodelcarmen.net) The charmingly surreal English version is less intelligible than Spanish, even if you don't speak a word of the latter!

Comunidad Valenciana tour~~ism~~ **authority** (www.comunitatva~~lenciana~~

LonelyPlanet.com (www~~.lonelyplanet~~.com) For travel informati~~on and~~ advice from other travel~~lers~~

This is Valencia (ww~~w~~

Valencia Conventi~~on~~

valencia.es)

Visit Valencia (~~

y 1 January
of the Three Kings)

Lost Property
Bus (☎ 96 315 85 15)
Metro (☎ 900 315851)
Train (☎ 96 353 71 90)

Metric System
Spain uses the metric system. Like the rest of Europe, except for the UK, Spaniards use commas in decimals and points to indicate thousands.

TEMPERATURE
$$°C = (°F - 32) ÷ 1.8$$
$$°F = (°C × 1.8) + 32$$

DISTANCE
1in = 2.54cm
1cm = 0.39in
1m = 3.3ft = 1.1yd
1ft = 0.3m
1km = 0.62 miles
1 mile = 1.6km

WEIGHT
1kg = 2.2lb
1lb = 0.45kg
1g = 0.04oz
1oz = 28g

VOLUME
1L = 0.26 US gallons
1 US gallon = 3.8L
1L = 0.22 imperial gallons
1 imperial gallon = 4.55L

Money
CURRENCY
Spain does its business in euros. There are seven notes in denominations of €500, €200, €100, €50, €20, €10 and €5. The eight euro coins come in denominations of €2, €1, €0.50, €0.20, €0.10, €0.05, €0.02 and €0.01.

TRAVELLERS CHEQUES
If you feel happier carrying an emergency, you're better off with a credit or debit card. Banks and exchange offices will accept travellers cheques to cash but you'll be stung if you try to use them for purchases and most hotels.

Amex (*Plaza de…*; ☎ 96 374 15 62; …represents American

CREDIT CARDS
Visa and MasterCard are widely accepted. Sometimes, especially in shops, you'll be asked for photo ID but scarcely ever will anyone glance at your signature. At modest hotels and restaurants, it's prudent to check in advance whether plastic's acceptable before you rack up a bill.

For 24-hour card cancellations or assistance contact the following numbers:
American Express (☎ 900 994426)
Diners Club (☎ 901 101011)
MasterCard (☎ 900 971231)
Visa (☎ 900 991124)

ATMS
ATMs are all over town. Look for *Telebanco* or *Servired* signs. If your card bears the Cirrus or Maestro logo and your credit's good, they'll happily spill notes out for you.

CHANGING MONEY
Banks, which abound, generally offer the fairest rates and lowest commissions. Valencia's few exchange offices (look for the *cambio* sign) open longer hours but may offer less favourable rates or slap on a hefty commission.

Newspapers & Magazines
The quality left-of-centre national newspaper *El País* brings out a daily Valencia edition. The two bestselling local dailies are *El Levante* and *Las Provincias*. Valencia's four competing free newspapers are handed out at transport hubs and around town. *Metro, 20 Minutos, Que?* and *El Micalet* are one of a kind – useful for checking what's on around town.

News Costa Levante is a recently introduced English-language weekly newspaper that carries some news about the city, has detailed satellite-TV listings and gives a fascinating glimpse into the world of resident Brit expats up and down the coast.

You can pick up the international press at several kiosks in and around Plaza del Ayuntamiento. For what's-on guides, s

Post

For more about **Correos** (2, C5; Plaza del Ayuntamiento 24; ⊗ 8.30am-8.30pm Mon-Fri, 9.30am-2pm Sat), Valencia's splendid central post office, see p24. Most tobacconists and all post offices sell stamps.

POSTAL RATES

Postage on a standard postcard or letter weighing up to 20g costs €0.28 within Spain, €0.53 within Europe, and €0.78 to the rest of the world.

Radio

In addition to a babble of local radio stations, the Spanish national network Radio Nacional de España (RNE) has several channels broadcasting nationwide. RNE 1 has general-interest and current-affairs programmes, RNE 2 plays classical music, RNE 3 has a great range of pop, rock and ethnic music, while RNE 5 is a round-the-clock news station. Among the most listened to commercial rock and pop stations are 40 Principales, Onda Cero and Cadena 100.

Telephone

Blue Telefónica phone booths are everywhere (though numbers are declining as callers rely more and more upon mobile phones). Nearly all accept both coins and Telefónica phonecards. Some will nibble at your credit card too.

PHONECARDS

A *tarjeta telefónica* (phonecard), valid for Telefónica phones, comes in €6 and €12 denominations. Pick one up at a tobacconist or post office. Quality varies but nowadays you'll get more chat for your euro by picking up a cut-rate scratch card from *locutorios* (call centres), plus many tobacconists and newsstands. *Locutorios*, often pitched at immigrant workers, also frequently offer cut-rate overseas calls.

MOBILE PHONES

Spain uses the GSM cellular *(movil)* phone system, compatible with most phones except those sold in Japan and the USA. Check whether your service provider has a roaming agreement with a Spanish counterpart. Using your home mobile phone can be an expensive activity; if you're a compulsive chatter, consider slipping in a Spanish SIM card, available for around €25.

COUNTRY & CITY CODES

The city code is an integral part of any phone number. Always include it, whether calling from next door or the other end of the world. Mobile-phone numbers usually begin with '6'.

USEFUL PHONE NUMBERS

International access code (☎ 00)
International directory inquiries (☎ 11825)
International operator – Europe (☎ 1008)
International operator – rest of world (☎ 1005)
International operator – national (☎ 11818)

Television

Terrestrial channels include TVE1 and La 2, both national services of state-run Televisión Española, and commercial stations Antena 3 and Tele 4, plus the dire Tele 5. Canal 9 and Punto 2 are Valencian public-sector channels, both massively subsidised by the local government and offering programmes in both Spanish and Valenciano.

These days, many even quite modest hotels will have cable or satellite TV offering international coverage and more channel than there are hours in the day.

Time

Valencia standard time is one hour of GMT/UTC. Clocks go forward by between the last Sunday in Ma last Sunday in October.

Timetables are usually e the 24-hour clock.

Tipping

Nobody expects you to tip in addition to restaurant service charges but a small extra (say, €1 per diner) will be well received. In bars, Spaniards often leave any loose change as a consideration. Tipping taxi drivers isn't common practice but you should dash the porter at a higher-end hotel.

Tourist Information

Valencia has five tourist offices that serve the city. Call ☎ 902 123212 for tourist information (at premium rates) or ring the individual office.

Diputación (Provincial) tourist office (2, D5; ☎ 96 351 49 07; www.valencia terraimar.org; Calle Poeta Querol s/n; 🕐 9.30am-7pm Mon-Fri, 10.30am-2pm Sat, 11.30am-2pm Sun) At the Teatro Principal.

Regional tourist office (2, E4; ☎ 96 398 64 22; www.comunitatvalenciana.com; Calle Paz 48; 🕐 9am-2.30pm & 4.40-8pm Mon-Fri) The best-informed.

Valencia Convention Bureau tourist office Plaza de la Reina (2, D4; ☎ 96 315 39 31; www.turisvalencia.es; Plaza de la Reina 19; 🕐 9am-7pm Mon-Sat, 10am-2pm Sun); Estación del Norte (2, C6; ☎ 96 352 85 73; 🕐 9am-9pm Mon-Sat, 10am-2pm Sun); Airport (☎ 96 153 02 29; arrivals area; 🕐 8.30am-8.30pm Mon-Fri, 9.30am-5.30pm Sat & Sun)

Women Travellers

There's a very real problem of domestic violence in Spain as a whole, but Valencia shouldn't present any specific difficulty female visitors. Younger Spaniards are ... less macho than their fathers and ... fathers and cases of harassment ... That said, exercise the same cau... you would in any city, especially ... ... d the contraceptive pill are ... le at pharmacies through-

LANGUAGE

The Comunidad Valenciana is officially bilingual. Everyone can understand Spanish, which is often called Castellano, meaning literally, the language of Castilla, the Spanish heartland up on the central plateau. Valenciano, the second official language is, according to strictly linguistic criteria, a dialect of Catalan, as is the mother tongue of many in Andorra, the Balearic Islands and even parts of Sardinia, where Alghero, a form of Catalan, clings on from the distant days when it belonged to Catalunya.

We've used standard (Castillian) Spanish in the following list of words and phrases, as just about everyone is at home speaking it. Where two alternatives are given, separated by a slash (eg asmático/a), it indicates the correct word to use depending on whether the speaker is male or female, respectively.

Basics

Hello.	¡Hola!
Goodbye.	¡Adiós!
Yes.	Sí.
No.	No.
Please.	Por favor.
Thank you.	Gracias.
You're welcome.	De nada.
Excuse me.	Perdón.
Sorry/Excuse me.	Lo siento/Discúlpeme.
Do you speak English?	¿Habla inglés?
I don't understand.	No entiendo.
How much is this?	¿Cuánto cuesta esto?

Getting Around

Where is (the metro station)?
¿Dónde está (la parada de metro)?
I want to go to...
Quiero ir a...
Can you show me (on the map)?
¿Me puede indicar (en el mapa)?
When does the ...leave/arrive?
¿A qué hora sale/llega el...?

bus	*autobús/bus*
train	*tren*
metro	*metro*

I'd like a ticket...
Quisiera un billete...

one-way	*sencillo*
return	*de ida y vuelta*

Accommodation

Do you have
¿Tiene

any rooms available?	*habitaciones libres?*
a single room	*una habitación individual*
a double room	*una habitación doble*
a room with a bathroom	*una habitación con baño*

How much is it...?
¿Cuánto cuesta...?

per night	*por noche*
per person	*por persona*

Around Town

I'm looking for...
Estoy buscando...

a bank	*un banco*
the cathedral	*la catedral*
the hospital	*el hospital*
the police	*la policía*

Eating

breakfast	*desayuno*
lunch	*comida*
dinner	*cena*
I'd like the set menu.	*Quisiera el menú del día.*
Is service included?	*¿La cuenta incluye servicio?*
I'm a vegetarian.	*Soy vegetariano/a.*

Time, Days & Numbers

What time is it?	*¿Qué hora es?*
today	*hoy*
tomorrow	*mañana*
yesterday	*ayer*
morning	*mañana*
afternoon	*tarde*
evening	*noche*
Monday	*lunes*
Tuesday	*martes*
Wednesday	*miércoles*
Thursday	*jueves*
Friday	*viernes*
Saturday	*sábado*
Sunday	*domingo*

0	*cero*
1	*uno/una*
2	*dos*
3	*tres*
4	*cuatro*
5	*cinco*
6	*seis*
7	*siete*
8	*ocho*
9	*nueve*
10	*diez*
100	*cien/ciento*
1000	*mil*

Health

I'm...
Soy...

diabetic	*diabético/a*
epileptic	*epiléptico/a*
asthmatic	*asmático/a*

I'm allergic to...
Soy alérgico/alérgica a...

antibiotics	*los antibióticos*
penicillin	*la penicilina*

Emergencies

Help!	*¡Socorro!*
Call a doctor!	*¡Llame a un médico!*
Call the police!	*¡Llame a la policía!*
Where are the toilets?	*¿Dónde están los servicios?*
Go away!	*¡Váyase!*
I'm lost.	*Estoy perdido/a.*

Index

See also separate subindexes for Eating (p93), Entertainment (p94), Shopping (p94), Sights with map references (p94) and Sleeping (p95)

FEATURES

Bar Pilar	*Eating*
Radio City	*Entertainment*
Turmix	*Drinking*
Estación del Norte	*Highlights*
Navarro	*Shopping*
Almudín	*Sights/Activities*
Ad Hoc	*Sleeping*

AREAS

- Beach, Desert
- Building
- Land
- Mall
- Market
- Other Area
- Park/Cemetery
- Sports
- Urban

HYDROGRAPHY

- River, Creek
- Intermittent River
- Canal
- Swamp
- Water

BOUNDARIES

- State, Provincial
- Regional, Suburb
- Ancient Wall

ROUTES

- Tollway
- Freeway
- Primary Road
- Secondary Road
- Tertiary Road
- Lane
- Under Construction
- One-Way Street
- Unsealed Road
- Mall/Steps
- Tunnel
- Walking Path
- Walking Trail/Track
- Pedestrian Overpass
- Walking Tour

TRANSPORT

- Airport, Airfield
- Bus Route
- Cycling, Bicycle Path
- Ferry
- General Transport
- Metro
- Monorail
- Rail
- Taxi Rank
- Tram

SYMBOLS

- Bank, ATM
- Beach
- Castle, Fortress
- Christian
- Diving, Snorkeling
- Embassy, Consulate
- Hospital, Clinic
- Information
- Internet Access
- Islamic
- Jewish
- Lighthouse
- Lookout
- Monument
- Mountain, Volcano
- National Park
- Parking Area
- Petrol Station
- Picnic Area
- Point of Interest
- Police Station
- Post Office
- Ruin
- Telephone
- Toilets
- Zoo, Bird Sanctuary
- Waterfall

24/7 travel advice
www.lonelyplanet.com